PÄIV
SANTE

Free as a
Global Nomad
An Old Tradition with a Modern Twist

DRIFTING SANDS PRESS • USA

Free as a Global Nomad:
An Old Tradition with a Modern Twist

Written by
Päivi Kannisto
Santeri Kannisto

Edited by
Cindie Cohagan

Published by
Drifting Sands Press
4022 East Evans Dr.
Phoenix, Arizona, USA
www.driftingsandspress.com

All translations and quotations from languages other than English have been made by the authors. Euros have been converted to US dollars using the exchange rate 1€ = $1.40. Exchange rates as of February 2011 have been applied to all other currencies.

ISBN 978-0-9850096-1-8 (Paperback)
ISBN 978-0-9850096-2-5 (eBook)

Printed in USA

Thanks to T (tevolving.com) and Arto Teräs (ajt.iki.fi)
for helping with the English language revision.

This book has received financial support from
the Finnish Association of Non-Fiction Writers.

Thank you so much,
Rita !
In Seattle on September
8, 2013

Table of Contents

Discovering Global Nomads 1

   Following the Great Masters 9

   Sex and Freeloading 17

   Guilty of Traveling 29

   The Great Escape 41

Life on the Road 49

   Freedom 65

   School of Life 75

   Exploring the Earth 85

   Travel Writing 93

Challenges 105

   Rootlessness 119

   Return 133

The Meaning of Life 143

Overview 151

   The Global Nomads 163

Select Bibliography 165

Discovering
Global Nomads

ONE MORNING IN KUALA LUMPUR, Malaysia, while having breakfast in a local restaurant, a Canadian man joined us at our table and told us his life story. He had been traveling for twenty-eight years and made his living repairing Ferrari cars and doing other odd jobs a few weeks out of every year. At the time, he was working as a doorman in a local brothel with plans to leave for West-Siberia with a friend.

We were at the beginning of pursuing a similar path. We had left our country of origin, Finland, a few years earlier to go traveling. It was a quick decision, although we had been brooding over it for some years. At the time, we knew nothing about the lifestyle we had chosen nor any other global nomads. We were intoxicated with the feeling that anything was possible and wholeheartedly enjoyed our new-found lifestyle, thinking perhaps we were the only ones who had solved the riddle of finding freedom.

We left Finland when we were both thirty-four years old. We had been working in business steaming ahead with our careers. I, Santeri, had a pioneering open source software company in Finland, Estonia, and Russia, while Päivi worked as a management consultant for one of the biggest corporations in Finland. Life was good. We were successful and happy, or at least others who considered material success to be the meaning of life, thought so.

When we met and fell in love, everything changed. After my second divorce, I threw a surprise party for the members of the Junior Chamber in my lavish house in Kauniainen, one of the most expensive neighborhoods in Greater Helsinki area. I invited Päivi, and when the text message arrived, she was sipping red wine in a lounge bar with a colleague. They didn't have to think twice about what to do. "Let's go," Päivi said, not anticipating where this spontaneous decision would eventually take her.

It was a warmish, quiet July night. Most Finns were in their summer cottages by the thousands of lakes that the country boasts about, but my house was ready for a wonderful evening. Sauna and swimming pool had been heated and the kitchen was full of booze: beer, whiskey, wine, liquor, and cigars. The house was decorated in a groovy '70s style— white functional building with great big windows—but it was under-furnished because my second wife had taken almost all furniture with her.

That evening Päivi and I started to talk more intimately. Although we had known each other for a year and a half, ours had been strictly a business relationship. "How is business going?" I asked. Päivi replied, "Swimmingly." Then with a desire to stop pretending she added, "I'm bored, I would like to quit and travel the world." "I've also had enough," I admitted. From that moment on, we started to look at each other in a different way and we were eager to learn more.

Soon we found ourselves kissing and moving upstairs. However, there wasn't much privacy in my house, so we decided to call a taxi and retire to Päivi's apartment. The next morning she took some of her clothes and toiletries along and moved into my house where some of the party-animals were still sleeping in the midst of empty liquor bottles.

The next three months we worked our normal jobs during the daytime, except on Mondays which we devoted to sex, red wine, good food, and a hot sauna, and in the evenings we developed our plan. We would leave everything we had and start exploring the world. The initial idea was to spend one year in three continents: South America, Africa, and Asia, but we quickly abandoned that idea. We didn't want to bind ourselves with long-term plans. Instead, we decided to buy plane tickets to Brazil where one of my former colleagues, Pedro, lived with his family. After visiting them, we would dance in the Samba Carnival in Rio de Janeiro which was a long-time dream of mine.

The decisions were quick and easy for us. The hardest part was telling our friends and family about our plans to leave. We anticipated there would be a lot of emotions and not just positive ones. We were not surprised to hear: "Are you crazy? Leaving your houses, cars and careers and hit the road? You must be out of your mind." Some predicted we would end up in the gutter after all our money was spent, while others admired our courage. After all, we had only started dating a couple of weeks earlier, which was of course another reason for worry. "How can you be sure that you will get along? Traveling is a hardy test for a relationship. If it doesn't work out, you'll have nothing to return to—no home, no job, nothing."

There was no point in explaining. We knew it would work. About the rest—well, we would see. We were tired of delaying our dreams for a better future as is expected in countries where the Protestant work ethic prevails. We wanted to act spontaneously and enjoy our life here and now when we were still young and able. What if we postponed our life to retirement years as most Westerners do, and died because of stress-related diseases before ever having a chance to live?

Our friends laughed at our reasoning. Most of them probably thought that our new career as globetrotters wouldn't last for long. They expected us to return to Finland after a couple of months to pursue our careers. For busy business people even a long weekend away from work might be too much. "You will lose the edge," we were warned.

What has happened to us? Eight years later we are still

traveling and don't have any plans to stop. Compared to our former life, status wise we are down in the gutter but in all honesty we couldn't be happier. We now look at ourselves as two meaningless particles in the vast universe.

People we have met have wondered what has kept us on the road, just as we were eager to know what had kept the Ferrari repairman we met in Kuala Lumpur on the road for almost thirty years. Our encounter kept haunting us for half a decade before we did something about it.

When we began to search for other global nomads in 2010, we soon discovered that there were no books about their lifestyle other than what individual travelers had written about their own adventures. Päivi found out that existing academic literature was not of help either as it focused on people who travel for other reasons than lifestyle—expatriates for work; lifestyle migrants for better climates, cheaper prices, and better quality of life; refugees and exiles for political asylum; ethnic minorities, such as gypsies and Irish travelers, to follow their century-old traditions, and tourists for leisure.

According to our own experiences, global nomads are on the move for the sake of travel rather than for wealth or a livelihood. Their motivation is immaterial rewards such as experiences, a simple life, and excitement. They search continuously for something new and do not necessarily want to settle down anywhere. They are people of many places but of no one place in particular.

Päivi started to call them global nomads. Nomads were pastoralists and warriors whose wandering is an ancient phenomenon. It started during the neolithic revolution when livestock economy began to develop and people settled down in villages. Ever since, nomads have intrigued the sedentary who have either feared or admired them. We suspected that our global nomads would rather travel alone or in pairs than with livestock and family, and instead of wilderness, they could be found in urban areas offering such services as accommodation, restaurants, supermarkets, and internet connections.

We contacted our friends and their friends and asked them for leads, and we plunged into social media sites and travel forums on the internet to spread the word. No ready networks were available as we soon discovered. Global nomads do not form communities.

The task proved to be challenging which, in all fairness, we knew beforehand it would be. We got leads for many interesting people but most of them had traveled only a year or two, or their travels were restricted to their home country. In addition, our messages in travel forums were censored, many of the prospects' e-mails bounced back, and some of the global nomads were not obsessed with internet at all and could not be contacted. Chance encounters such as ours in Kuala Lumpur were rare as global nomads usually avoid touristy areas.

We were determined to continue, however, and wanted to draw a 360 degree picture of the lifestyle. Who are global nomads? How do they travel? Why did they leave their former lives? Will they return to those lives? How do they finance their travels? And—ultimately—what is the meaning of life for them?

Following the Great Masters

We found most of the global nomads, among them forty-nine-year-old American Phoenix, with the help of other global nomads. When we contacted Phoenix, he was living in Texas where he grew up. Texas never really felt like home to him. His family is originally from Greece and a beach lifestyle of skateboarding and surfing in California is what he dreamed about the most.

When Phoenix was eighteen, he saved three hundred dollars and bought a plane ticket to San Francisco. The instant he got out of the plane, he felt the vibrating energy of the city. Phoenix had never seen anything so beautiful: he instantly fell in love with the mist coming down from the mountains.

Phoenix was just a kid when he arrived, lonely and shy, and he had only five dollars left in his pocket. He wanted to become a writer and started living on the streets to gather life experiences. To this day he remembers the intense experience he had at the Richmond Rescue Mission.

"I went crazy," Phoenix says laughing, referring to his sudden decision to join the Marines. He spent three years in Japan, Korea, and the Philippines living in the jungle and tracking down revolutionaries. After serving his time, he didn't continue his military career, but returned to the United States. There he lived in a '67 Volkswagn bug, went rock climbing, played in a band, and met a girl.

Phoenix couldn't be stationary for long. Soon he became involved in human rights activities and traveled to Central America. He said good-bye to his girlfriend at the US border with Mexico and from there the trip continued southwards with the help of some magic mushrooms. On his two and a half year journey through Latin America, Phoenix visited the same places as Che Guevara did. Phoenix was also the same age as Che and as penniless. He was in Nicaragua for the war and Panama for the uprisings.

After Latin America it was India that called Phoenix next. He studied yoga and ayurvedic medicine, rock climbed in Nepal and hiked in the Himalayas. Since then, he has gone on to teach yoga and ayurvedic medicine. Yoga is an integral part of Phoenix's daily life. He gets up early every morning, meditates, and does his yoga and breathing exercises. Then he sits outside in the backyard sipping a cup of tea. Yoga has taught Phoenix what he really wants: to live in harmony with his values. He had recently turned down a lucrative job offer. In the end he didn't want to teach English to foreign soldiers so that they could go and make war.

Phoenix says hunger is the best motivator. When his stomach was gnawing, he found an incredible amount of talents in himself. He performed in bars playing guitar and singing, taught English classes, wrote dispatches for an international press, set up community projects, and opened an underground club in Argentina.

When we first talked with Phoenix in 2010, he was studying for a master's degree at the University of Texas. His thesis was almost finished and after that he planned to go to Japan and New Zealand to teach English as a second language. New Zealand is where Phoenix feels the most at home. If he could, he would like to make it his home country.

Phoenix lives modestly in his van in the USA. He proudly shows us his mobile home where he has everything he needs: his electric guitar and his massage table. Phoenix loves to live outdoors and in rhythm with nature. Sleeping on the beach under the stars suits him the best. However, his family is worried about him and wishes he had taken another life path. At fifty, Phoenix doesn't have much money, professional career, or immediate family. His parents are afraid that he is going to die homeless and in the gutter. Quite surprisingly, many of Phoenix's friends are also worried about him. But at the same time they see him as a bit of an icon, someone who is willing to live the way they always dreamed of living but were afraid to try. He is a sort of a romantic warrior for them.

When Phoenix has a dream, he goes for it, and by the time he has actualized that dream he is off after a new dream. He has spent his life going from one dream to next. Sometimes he plans, because it is nice to have plans, but most of the time he doesn't have a plan at all. He will be the first to admit that he doesn't always know what to do next.

At the end of our conversation, we notice the rain is dancing on the roof of Phoenix's van, and the birds are singing. It feels like time has melted away and become meaningless. "Heaven is where you find it," Phoenix muses. He takes out his guitar and starts playing.

How does Phoenix's journey relate to his predecessors, the great masters of the art of traveling? Phoenix's wanderlust was nurtured by stories he read when he was young. He read about the world's great explorers and dreamed of foreign countries, scuba-diving, and sky-diving. As a teenager he also had a mad love affair with France. He read a lot of Hemingway and fancied living the European literary and intellectual life.

Once Phoenix got started traveling, he just couldn't stop. His reasons for traveling have been varied. While revolutionaries took him to Latin America and yoga to India, his interest in ancient history and mythology led him to Turkey. Phoenix followed in the footsteps of Alexander the Great

(356–323 BC), who was one of the most well-traveled men of his time. In little more than a decade, Alexander the Great journeyed further than any single person before him and expanded his empire from Greece to India.

It is not uncommon for global nomads to follow the example of famous travelers. Päivi discovered in her research that these ancestors created an image of what traveling should be like, what kind of experiences and events were to be expected, and how one's self was going to develop. Alexander the Great set a unique example for generations to come. Travels, for him, were victories like the Arabian proverb states as every journey expanded his empire. During his reign, Alexander founded seventy cities in Africa and Western Asia, many of which were named after him. The great conqueror's dream was to create a kingdom that would be ruled according to one set of principles. Some historians consider Alexander's imperialism as an early step towards globalism.

Traveling was a necessity for Alexander as a means to expand his realm, accumulate wealth and prove his superiority, but did he enjoy traveling? The great leader and his troops encountered many hardships on their way. In the desert, they suffered from lack of water and they often got lost. Alexander ignored his own sufferings or rather drew his inspiration from them. He was a predecessor of the Romantic traveler who not only encountered dangers bravely but sought them out. Accidents, risks, and close calls encouraged him to continue.

This ideal still exists and some global nomads imitate it, consciously or unconsciously. In Phoenix's story the past and the present of the nomadic lifestyle entwine seamlessly. "I lead a very romantic life, I can't deny that," Phoenix says and adds in the spirit of suffering Romantics: "I've spent more nights lying in freezing mud or snow, steaming jungles, ditches, trenches, with things crawling over me, had more tropical diseases, been through more hardships and almost lost my life more times than anybody would want to even think about. I have bullet holes, knife holes, burn scars. You might say I've earned my twenty years of alternative living the hard way."

Among the more recent traveler icons is American author Jack Kerouac who created a cult of hitchhiking and rebellion against middle-class respectability in his book *On the Road* (1957). Kerouac inspired the young to leave home in order to travel like Romantic misadventurers: to expose themselves to uncertainties and difficulties and grow up in the process. Kerouac himself chose another path. He found the meaning of life in binge drinking which eventually killed him.

Most of the icons are conquerors, bohemians, artists, and explorers, and all travelers have their own favorites. Päivi remembers from her childhood Doctor Livingstone who—in her mind—was paddling through the Amazon rainforest wearing a white panama hat. This image was most probably a combination of various real and imaginative explorers as David Livingstone didn't really explore Brazil but Africa.

Spiritual wanderers have equally served as role models. Phoenix was attracted to yoga and ayurvedic medicine and traveled in India where wandering has a long history. The tradition of sadhus, homeless Indian wanderers practicing Hinduism, dates back almost three thousand years. Alexander the Great sought sadhus' advice and Buddha followed their practices to renounce suffering. In the 1930s, before India gained independence, Mahatma Gandhi spread his anti-caste message dressed in a sadhu robe.

By wandering, sadhus try to free themselves of mundane attachments. They believe that time, place, space, and the world around us are immaterial illusions, and it is the sedentary lifestyle which keeps the body trapped in these daily spheres and the mind immersed in a web of human desires and sufferings.

Wandering has been part of all major religions—Buddhism, Christianity, Hinduism, and Islam—but sadhu tradition is one of the rare ones that still continues till this day. Monastic communities have not tied sadhus down nor has wandering been reduced to short pilgrimages in the name of efficiency.

In the Christian world, one of the most famous pilgrimage routes is El Camino de Santiago in Spain which is popular among Christians and non-Christians alike. Yoga teacher Phoenix hiked it and dreams of going there again.

In religious texts, traveling can refer to a concrete pilgrimage or a metaphorical journey focusing on inner growth. The wanderers of the Old Testament, for instance, were often on hellish trips from a lost paradise to the promised land, or from the earthly abode to the heavenly. When the conditions of the former home country became unbearable, people had to start looking for other opportunities. Today, these journeys would probably be called immigration.

Biblical exodus had, however, an added feature compared to its materially driven counterpart. The journey also emphasized hardship which demonstrated suffering for the sake of Christ. The more hardships travelers encountered, the surer it was God had blessed them. Were they Romantic travelers following Alexander the Great's example, awaiting misadventures? Probably not, as they were cast to traveling reluctantly. They were passive participants of divine plots rather than action-seeking heroes.

In Christianity wandering became a popular practice during the Roman empire in late antiquity, in the fifth and sixth centuries. Monks embraced poverty and ventured out into the deserts of Syria and Egypt. They were inspired by a literal interpretation of certain passages of the New Testament in which Jesus was described as a homeless vagrant who had nowhere to lay his head. He took the most despicable human form and, by thus humbling himself, brought salvation to all humanity. The vagrant became a hero, a savior.

Christian monks wanted to imitate Jesus and his apostles. This required absolute poverty, homelessness, constant prayer, and study of religious teachings. Their goal was to free themselves from material and social circumstances which might hinder their ability to trust in God.

Are you here to find God?
I didn't know he was lost.
—Hobo Andy

As various religious wanderers show, there is nothing new in global nomads' roaming. Wandering has been considered a beneficial practice since immemorial times. This has led to outwardly similar kinds of practice—constant movement and asceticism—regardless of the religion. The underlying philosophical premises, however, might vary, although there are more similarities than differences. All major religions ultimately revered the same ideals: detachment from material and social ties and a simple life leading to spiritual growth.

For most global nomads spiritualism is neither an aim nor a reason for starting to travel—neither was it for us. Yet, spiritualism gave us invaluable insights on the nomadic lifestyle. It contextualizes some of the changes that wandering can trigger. Getting rid of material possessions has in many religions a deeper, spiritual meaning than just having a lighter backpack to carry. Whereas monks showed their trust in God by getting rid of their possessions, global nomads might show their dislike of continuous economic growth, consumerist values, generation of waste, pollution, and the disasters that follow with getting rid of their possessions.

Like other world travelers, I have been shocked by the state of the earth and want to consume as little as possible. I have often pondered why I needed all that junk I had in Finland. If the aim was to make my life easier, it sure didn't help. Life without all those garage loads of stuff is not only possible but even desirable, like a heavy burden lifted off my shoulders. If I sometimes missed an odd item in the beginning of our trip, I soon figured out a clever way to do without. With less material things, creativity is unleashed.

Another similarity in the lifestyle of wandering monks and global nomads alike is geographical detachment. Global nomads rarely stay in one place for a long time. Constant moving detaches them from a local point of view and teaches open-mindedness, flexibility, and compassion for people who live in other ways.

I believe that religious wanderers did have a point. It does no harm for anyone to leave familiar surroundings and comforts for some time no matter how it's done—wandering in the desert enjoying the proximity of death, following the teachings of old masters, or hooking up with like-minded souls.

How long is enough? Is a one or two-week pilgrimage enough to get rid of routines and old models of thinking? Probably not. For us, it has taken years and we still feel we are carrying a lot of unnecessary baggage in our minds. Although we have managed to get rid of most of our material possessions, mental waste requires much more effort. One of our American nomads described this ever ongoing process well. Like us, he tries to simplify his life and see the core reality of everything. "I'm trying to strip away everything that is not necessary. Probably ninety per cent of what we do is scripted," he related.

The scripted consists of habits and beliefs we have adopted from home, school, university, work, the media, and our circle of friends. It might have been valid in the context where it was learned, but could become absurd or even harmful in other situations. Global nomads realize the effects of the scripted in their lives when comparing and experiencing different philosophies of life, different customs, and different cultures side by side. By shedding their own cultural baggage and adopting new ways of living they can make a journey that is both an inner and outer discovery. However, there are no guarantees in life. Even if you follow in somebody's footsteps, like those of the old great masters, you might have a totally different experience.

Sex and Freeloading

Why do global nomads leave their countries of origin? For global nomads, traveling is natural and from their point of view the question should be rephrased: Why do people get stuck in one place? When so many people dream of traveling, why do only a few do it? Questions like: "Why travel?" and "Why stay?" reflect different approaches to life. Eventually they are entwined because they are different sides of the same thing. All global nomads have at some point been stationary and they will also stay put for some periods of time during their travels.

Twenty-nine-year old Canadian Anick, whom we found through a hospitality exchange network, answered the above questions. Anick's travels began like many other students': she studied one year abroad. That was about all she had in common with other students. She first settled in Scotland and then in continental Europe, but not just in one city or country. She has spent time in Great Britain, France, Germany, and the Netherlands, but not living anywhere in particular. Instead, Anick knows people and she knows where she can stay. The places she feels most at home are Edinburgh, Scotland, Berlin,

Germany and Montreal, Canada.

Anick was born on one of the Magdalen Islands, Quebec, Canada. She studied Health and Safety in college and continued with Biophysics at university. She never dreamed of traveling, unlike other global nomads. She describes herself as a utilitarian filling in her CV. By traveling she wanted to do something exceptional—show that she can deal with tricky situations and learn something new. Opportunities have taken Anick to various places. She volunteered in Peru to learn Spanish, and she went to Germany because she had an intuition that she would get married to a German.

Anick tried to settle down in one place, but she became depressed and realized that fitting into a regular lifestyle and having a long-term job didn't fit her mentality. Anick speculated possible reasons for her desire for a nomadic lifestyle: was it her personality, inability to manage stress properly, her experiences, or the rhythm of society? The result remained the same. All these things together didn't seem to keep her healthy.

Anick was sure that if she didn't force things, she would feel when it was the right time to settle down. Lately, however, she has realized that the right time doesn't seem to be coming so she had better make some changes. Settling down is not her goal anymore. She wants to develop herself professionally, and for that traveling offers a very condensed opportunity.

Personal development is important for Anick—sometimes even more important than a couple relationship. If she is on the road and something catches her attention, she wants to be able to take that chance. She can't imagine herself traveling or being with someone a very long time. She prefers open relationships.

Anick travels alone because she has her own style. She hitchhikes and the longest trip so far has taken her from western Europe to Turkey. "It is difficult to compromise and cope with another person's ways of not coping," she says. The main thing that annoys Anick when traveling with other people is their moodiness. When they are hungry, they get cravings and their moods shift. It is also difficult to make decisions about which route to take and what time to leave. Traveling together requires some thinking ahead and some global nomads are reluctant to do any planning. Anick tried it with a few guys she was interested in, but soon realized that finding a balance between compromise and sacrifice was hard. In fact, for the same reasons as Anick, we rejected the idea of traveling with other global nomads when writing this book.

A single and childless traveler invites curiosity on the road, particularly in family-oriented cultures. In Muslim countries Anick has sometimes had to say she is married, although then locals started to wonder who is doing all the housework when Madame is just traveling around. Anick's mother is sometimes afraid for her. A young woman alone is easily viewed as a target for various ill intentions. Single women are at least being hit on, especially in Third World countries where men chase Western women for their money or to get married and out of their country, or simply for sex.

Sex is one of the most powerful drivers in life. It can motivate nomadic travels by influencing the choice of destinations or by giving a purpose to otherwise aimless wandering. The lack of a permanent partner can drive a person to short relationships, buying sex, or abstinence. Anick has had various relationships and breakups which have guided her way through Europe.

Like Anick, some other global nomads have chosen to go solo, but traveling alone is not always the preferred way. It might be more of a reality as finding travel companion is difficult. One of our American nomads, who is currently without a partner, admits loneliness is the hardest to endure over the long run. Although he has had successful relationships, he has never been in a situation where there was a special person who could travel with him. He estimates that the odds of finding someone of similar interests, someone open-minded enough, and someone who he is attracted to, are astronomically low.

Obviously nomad men and women don't meet each other. Both represent a rare minority, and because of their mobility, the probability to meet is indeed small. Some global nomads think that relationships tied on the road wouldn't even work. Relationships are complicated enough on their own not to mention if both parties are travelers. The traveler's mindset is that they are free. If something doesn't work out, one or the other will just pick up and leave.

Some men suggest that the root problem lies in the small number of women on the road. However, we found that female nomads talk about the challenge of finding a partner just like men: boyfriends are not always adventurers either, willing to leave their home, work, mother, and their circle of friends.

We find traditional gender roles guiding men to be like the lone rangers in the old westerns and women to be home-makers artificial and limiting, and fortunately there is no need to conform to them nor strengthen them. Päivi never fit the traditional image of a child-loving and family-centered woman which sometimes caused friction for her in Finland. I was a safe partner for her as I already had children from two previous marriages. Life on the road has saved us from further questioning about our married life.

I have often been judged for abandoning my children. The idea of children needing a stable living environment and both parents is probably so inscribed in people's minds that nobody questions it. Indeed, the decision wasn't an easy one to make. I could have stayed around, kept working to pay taxes and alimony, and be there for my children whenever their mothers would have let them see me. By staying, however, I would have given my children an example of sacrificing my own life and happiness. In the worst case my children would have followed my example later and ended up being unhappy as well.

I have often witnessed the fact that promoting something

is the surest way to drive people to do the opposite. So it was this time as well. My daughter told me in spring 2012 that she will have a baby. When I published the news on Facebook and said that I would have rather seen my daughter first considering to adopt one of the sixteen million AIDS orphans in Africa instead of having her own baby, I opened a can of worms. People were horrified and claimed that my attitude was sick. From my point of view, there is already way too many people on earth polluting our planet and murdering animals for food and products.

Societies and communities are based on numerous unwritten norms which direct people's conduct and their choices. All deviations require explanation whether they concern being single or in a relationship, having or not having children, staying put or wandering. Everyone of us carries the normal in ourselves. It is the scripted, the internalized concept that tells us how we should live our lives. We used to comply with the norms of Finnish society by climbing the career ladder and acquiring signs of status. I also adhered to the norms of family life by having children and a poor-bred dog. I had internalized the scripted models so thoroughly that they felt natural to me as if they had been born out of my own desires. In hindsight, I was like an obedient child who wants to please others by achieving, and I craved recognition in return.

Even people who consider themselves open-minded are tied to norms as we experienced in a Rainbow hippie camp in Karelia, Russia. Participants were mostly vegetarians who disapproved of drinking but smoked weed. Nudity was more a rule than an exception, and everyone was expected to wear colorful handmade beads. We had none, so our neighbors made us armbands so that we would blend in better. I learned that it was essential to be open-minded in the same way as everyone else: wear beads, be naked, and smoke weed.

The nomadic lifestyle causes strong reactions—condemntion, anger, admiration, and envy—because it questions many of societies' norms. Aimless drifting is an enigma which outsiders try to solve by digging up nomads' real motives. Whenever we have been unwilling to give meanings to our journey, others have done it for us. This behavior is presented intriguingly in the French film *Vagabond* (1985), directed by Agnès Varda. It made me think of Anick.

In the film, a young vagabond woman, Mona, is represented solely from the outside. The camera interviews people Mona met during her travels, whilst her own thoughts, background and motives are not revealed.

The film begins when Mona's tormented frozen body is found in the gutter. In flashbacks, the camera shows her wandering alone in little villages, hitchhiking carelessly on the roadsides, idling in construction sites and vineyards with shady migrant workers, and staying in a goat farm with a hard-working hippie family. The camera follows her and interviews people she met in a documentary style. Mona never tells her life story nor explains her choices, which leaves the interpretations to the spectator. Did Mona choose her vagabond existence or was her life just going down the drain? The question inevitably leads to another: what is deemed useful? Is our life useful if we work every day, consume to keep national economies rolling, maintain sometimes forced relationships with our relatives, colleagues and neighbors, and root ourselves in our community?

Anick has not tied herself to turf, but she would like to contribute to the knowledge on earth and at the same time organize her thoughts and achieve something tangible. Like yoga teacher Phoenix, she prefers to work on something which is consistent with her values. She doesn't believe she can save the world, but she tries to bring environmental consciousness to her practices and to her circle of friends.

For Anick and us alike, the idea of being tied down to a full-time work in one country and city is not tempting. We prefer to earn and consume less to keep our freedom. Downshifting is a personal choice that has effects on a small scale to ourselves and to those close to us; on a national and global scale, however, downshifting would mean the end of national economies. Why? The growth of an economy requires debt since it is debt that fuels the creation of new money. This means that people have to be encouraged to consume more than they earn so that they have to borrow money. Mostly debt-free and low-consuming global nomads do not participate in these growth orgies.

Are global nomads freeloaders? The answer depends on which values and priorities it is based on. If the goal is eternal growth of an economy, everyone leaving the system is a freeloader. Citizens are expected to contribute to and increase the general standard of living. However, if the aim is to reduce consumption to a more sustainable level, global nomads are on the right track. Instead of growth, a radical reduction in consumption is needed, or preferably negative growth, in order to avoid catastrophes like Chernobyl, Fukushima, and the Gulf of Mexico oil spill, and to stop contributing to the climate change that is annihilating life on earth. The more goods are produced, the more our globe is beginning to resemble a giant junkyard.

Visiting China was an eye-opening experience for me. In cities, the sky was always gray, and our lungs and skin were quickly irritated by pollution. I doubt that even the most nationalistic can claim that air pollution respects borders. The winds spread it all over the world. Many Western companies have their products made in China because it is cheaper giving them higher profits. In China, they don't have to care about polluting environment nor treating their workers well. Every time we buy these products, we approve what they are doing and help them to contaminate our planet and abuse their workers.

Then, one day, when we were sitting in a Chinese railway station waiting for the train, I observed people passing by and got another insight on the most vexing environmental issue today. We were sitting near a trash can and I noticed how every piece of trash was diligently inserted into the right slot of recyclables. Then came the janitor to collect the trash and he emptied all the trash into the same bag. After witnessing this numerous times in numerous countries, I realized that recycling, for the most part, is just a scam to keep us consuming and feeding the growth.

Because growth is one of the key values in Western societies, downshifting seems wrong or at least backward to many. I am often asked, "What would happen if everyone else did the same, worked and consumed less, or just traveled without being productive and contributing to society?" The question reflects the fear that the example of idling is infectious and poisons the minds of other people. It is also a rhetorical question because not everyone will ever do the same. The nomadic lifestyle as a permanent or even as a temporary phase of life will never be mainstream.

What the argument against freeloading fails to take into account is that global nomads work for their living, or they live on their hard-earned or inherited savings. They are not exploiting other people's resources nor social security of any country. Yet, the question of freeloading is intriguing because it reveals the primary position the monetary economy has in our lives. Everything is measured in money, be it our work efforts or our value as a human beings. We are what we own. Even the value of a happy relationship has been calculated in money. In this respect I'm super rich, but fortunately the tax man hasn't realized it.

I have chosen to live outside the economy. I have no money, no bank account, and I don't possess anything valuable. In my life I have seen money cause only bad things and I wouldn't give it to anyone, not even to my worst enemy. Money turns all good things in life into bad. I'm happy to work but only if I don't have to accept a salary. Päivi gets some money from our books and that gives us the option of using other means of travel than walking. I'm ready to return to the economy as soon as there is something meaningful to buy like world peace.

In a money-oriented society global nomads are strange outcasts. Why would anyone forgo job opportunities that would earn them a fortune, or why would they leave all their possessions behind like I did? Whenever I have been unable to reason our never-ending honeymoon logically, others have given me innovative business ideas such as buying guitars and cow hides in New Zealand and selling them abroad for a huge profit, or writing about the destinations we have visited for newspapers and glossy magazines.

Instead of working just for money, I want to spend my time meaningfully. Independence and freedom to go whenever, wherever are more important for me. Global nomads also use other currencies than money such as giving and sharing. Anick volunteered for a hospitality exchange organization for three years. She was not paid for the work but she was able to show to others that she had an occupation.

Work can also be done in exchange for food and accommodation at farms and construction sites like in the old days. We have experienced both. In France, we assisted two of our friends in building an ecological house from straw bales, and the second time we helped another friend with remodeling work including painting and installing new electrical wiring. In Borneo, Malaysia, we lived on a chilli farm for four months helping our host tend to the farm and do house maintenance in exchange for room. In our free time we were writing this book.

Because many global nomads travel in Third World countries, downsizing and reducing living costs by the cheaper price levels in those countries raises an ethical question: Is it right that people who have made big money in wealthy Western countries exploit the low prices in poor countries? Should they pay more than locals? This question comes up often with short-term travelers as well. Anick related a story about her visit to a Peruvian slum. An old woman seized her hand and yelled at her: "You gringita, you are rich, you have millions and millions," to which Anick replied: "No, but I have a student loan of twenty thousand."

The association of foreigners and wealth is ancient and prevalent, and it can cause various scruples. Where to draw the line between enjoying generosity as a guest and exploiting one's host? In tourism industry, a fair financial transaction is viewed to benefit the host community. Shoestring travelers, that most nomads represent, are often criticized for saving money, haggling over prices, and hunting for bargains. Among other travelers, however, traveling on a low budget is often a matter of honor. Those who spend the least money are considered to be the most hardcore as traveling with little money requires resourcefulness and endurance.

Anick enjoys the reputation of a hard-core traveler in her circles. She is considered an interesting person to hang out with which has raised her social status. She believes this image also contributes to her ability to inspire other people. Anick herself denies being that hard-core and admits that it is sometimes difficult to be social around people who admire her. People see her lifestyle as romantic. Anick prefers to travel with truck drivers because they see her as an ordinary person. They don't need to know everything about her. They prefer to talk about themselves, the places they have been to, and what they think about other people.

People who want to buy a dream, live vicariously through Anick's lifestyle. They sometimes will give Anick donations. Many of them are Canadians who would like to leave the rat race behind but for whatever reason are not ready to make the move. Anick is glad for the opportunity of being grateful, but reminds us that the dreams people nurture are not her reality. There are downsides as well. Sometimes Anick has to go hungry and walk twenty-five miles (forty kilometers) because she doesn't have a ride. She might be tired and sick, and still she has to go to a new place and constantly take care of herself.

Who benefits, from whom, and how much in financial transactions is always a disputable question. When talking about the subject, it is good to keep in mind the aim of the discussion. Is the speaker a politician who wants the economy to grow in the short-term to get more votes; is it a local entrepreneur who wants to get as much profit as possible with minimal work; is it a bum who refuses to work for living; or an ecological consumer to whom the environment is more important than his own comfort?

Another thing to be remembered is that many of the sensations traveling has to offer are free and do not require anyone to pay anything—neither are they taking anything away from somebody else. Encountering altruistic kindness is one of the pleasures of traveling. Getting a lift from a stranger and an invitation to be his guest is a gesture of trust and respect which leaves me in awe every time it happens. It is like a blessing for those of us who have tumbled through the hard, icy society.

Guilty of Traveling

Hospitality exchange services (hospex) such as BeWelcome, CouchSurfing, Hospitality Club and Servas are important resources for global nomads. Although there are no nomadic communities, many global nomads are members of these services. We joined one in 2006, and well before writing this book we opened a discussion group for long-term travelers to exchange experiences and trade tips. The group proved to be a good source for finding global nomads despite the fact that eighty per cent of the members were only interested in a short-term nomadic lifestyle. They were dreaming about a one or two-year sabbatical or a round-the-world tour, but few would come to realize their journeys.

Soon after talking with Anick, one of the members of a hospex contacted us. He needed a place to stay for a night. When reading his profile, I realized he was a global nomad. I got excited and wanted to meet him, but I didn't have our landlord's permission to host. Instead, I directed him to contact a friend of ours who was also a member in the same organization. Marco gladly promised to host him, and he also threw a party for the local hospex community in his house so that we got all a chance to meet Anthony.

Thirty-five-year-old Belgian Anthony was casually dressed in jeans and a T-shirt when we met him. He had not shaved for a couple of days and he certainly didn't look like a typical business school graduate from the prestigious Solvay Business School in Belgium. Anthony was a global nomad who had visited all the 192 countries in the world recognized by the United Nations. In 2005, he founded an organization called "Art in All of Us." Through that organization, Anthony visits schools creating drawings and taking photographs with children. These activities aim to promote tolerance and creative cultural exchange. Although it was curiosity that initially drove Anthony to travel, the organization provides him with a legitimate reason to travel in the eyes of others.

Anthony invested his savings into his NGO (non-governmental organization) and searched for partners to join him. It was hard at first, because he didn't have any experience or financial support. He was consistently told to come back in two to three years after he had experience. Eventually the UN backed his project, and finding support for his work became easier.

From Anthony's calendar one could assume he is a busy businessman: it is fully booked months ahead. School visits require a lot of planning and negotiations. Usually Anthony has to start to work with a school three to nine months before the visit. In Turkmenistan, Anthony needed a parliamentary decision to work in the country, and with a North-Korean school the negotiations took two and a half years.

The visit to North-Korea became one of the highlights of Anthony's traveling career. North-Korean children receive no information about other countries. There is no internet and the television only shows programs accepted by the political elite.

The classroom burst with excitement when Anthony presented a map of the world. The pupils had only seen a map of North-Korea. One of them asked if there were also children in his country and if they were communists, too. "For him, it was the same kind of question as asking if people in Belgium were happy," Anthony explained. Another child told him that he would like to build high-rises because then he would be able to see a friend of his who is living in South-Korea.

Anthony was surprised by the spontaneity of the situation and the honesty of the children. Teachers were monitoring the class and all of the children's questions and answers were translated. If the visit was staged, the children must have been professional actors.

Anthony is not entirely happy with his busy schedule. He can only stay one or two days in his destinations and then he is off to the next one. Staying longer would ruin his plans, flights, visas—everything. When visiting the world's smallest island state, Nauru, there was only one flight available. Anthony had to spend either an indefinite amount of time on the island or return on the same plane. He decided to take the chance even though he had not agreed a meeting beforehand.

The airplane landed on the island's main street which served as a runway. In immigration Anthony's passport was withheld, as is the custom, and he was told that he could fetch it from the Minister of Defense two days later. Anthony was flabbergasted as he had no time to wait, but luckily, after a discussion with the officials, he was promised an express service.

After clearing immigration, the visit went quickly. The third passer-by in the street knew the teacher and the Minister of Education lent his car to Anthony so that he could go to meet the pupils. The teacher was woken up from her neighbor's hammock, the pupils were summoned to class room, and the Minister of Energy organized electricity for the night so that they could work. At one o'clock at night all children were taken back home, Anthony got his passport from the Minister who was in his pajamas, and he ran to the airport to catch his plane.

When we met in Sicily, Italy, Anthony had just paid a surprise visit to his godchild. He has friends all over the world and he tries to see them as often as possible. But is there anything to see after 192 countries, we wondered.

"Definitely. I've been thirty times in Brazil, but I always want to go back. One day I might settle down there, or in Columbia, but not yet. I still have work to do," Anthony smiled and disappeared to his host's coach to take a couple of hours' nap before the other guests arrived. He had an early flight to Belgium the next morning.

How did the business school graduate become a footloose wanderer? What is it about rough traveling that fascinates intelligent young people like Anthony? Full-time traveling is hard work and its image is often dubious. While some people revere nomads as courageous adventurers, others despise them as worthless vagrants. We witnessed both reactions for the first time when we told our friends and families about our decision to leave. The same stories have followed us everywhere. We are sometimes interviewed for the media because of our cool lifestyle, but much more often we are treated as suspicious vagrants like one night when we ended up in Taormina railway station in Sicily, Italy.

We had slept in and missed our train. As there were no trains running that night, we decided to put our sleeping mattresses on the benches and sleep. Early in the morning a *carabinieri*, an Italian policeman, woke me up and asked which train we were going to take. I had no idea about the schedule so I consulted the timetable on the wall and noticed that we would have to wait for a couple more hours. After getting a reason for us hanging out in the train station, the policeman let us stay and moved on to a couple of gypsies who were playing violins on the platform. They were thrown out of the train station.

I failed to understand what danger did two well-behaved foreign travelers and a merry group of gypsy musicians pose to an otherwise empty railway station, but Päivi had studied that throughout time, full-time traveling has been associated with society's outcasts: vagrants, tramps, beggars, gypsies, con men, and bohemians. They have stirred up negative feelings in their sedentary counterparts, and still do.

Vagrants were mostly seasonal agricultural workers or professionals of rare trades. Their counterparts—beggars, con men, and criminals—avoided work and preferred to beg, steal and swindle instead. Since the Middle Ages, Western societies have had a difficult time drawing the line between the two. Who really needed and deserved assistance, and who were merely exploiting the system?

In England between the fifteenth and mid-sixteenth centuries, officials restricted all underclass wanderings regardless of the reasons for their loitering. As a result, vagrants were arrested and sentenced only because they had no home or job, while murderers and killers were punished because of the crime they had committed. Aimless wandering thus became a crime.

The arrested were sent to workhouses and prisons. The treatment was harsh: corporal punishment, loss of freedom, and compulsory labor. Vagrants were branded with a "v" on their chest, they were whipped, their ears were perforated and hair shaved. Publicly dunking people in the river or leaving them in a pillory in the town square made sure that offenders were exposed to public scorn.

Compulsory labor reigned. Laws required that all the poor who were able to work had masters. Dependent workers, servants and apprentices, formed the bulk of the labor-force who floated from job to job. On average, vagrants traveled 70–80 miles (110–130 kilometers) a month living in pubs and sleeping outside.

Vagrancy was despised as immoral and it was viewed to be the fault of the person, not society's. Vagrants were considered a menace to the public order and morality as authorities feared that the bad example would spread. Leisure time or loitering was accepted only for the rich whereas the poor had to work to earn their living as the Bible taught: "You will eat bread by the sweat of your brow."

Work was valued above all else in North America, England, and other protestant North-European countries, because work was viewed as a way to get to heaven. Worldly success was believed to guarantee success in afterlife just like good deeds and indulgences brought salvation to the Catholics. The same mentality that worships work can still be seen in social work. Studying and working are believed to be the best ways to reintegrate the alienated young people into society. This approach insinuates that society only wants and accepts those members it deems useful. Others who do not study or work remain outcasts.

A vivid example of the ways in which fear of strangers have been created can be seen in the history of vagrancy. The threat of vagrancy worked like the threat of terrorism today. Citizens were made to provide voluntary information about themselves and others to authorities, and by frightening the middle and the upper class, various products and services that provided them with the illusion of security could be sold at a profit.

Vagrants of old arose suspicions which global nomads cannot escape either. Like their shady predecessors, they lack the familiar anchors of home, address, and a permanent job. They can be taken for poor and homeless, bums and free-loaders, con men and drug dealers, tax refugees and other fugitives. I experienced this first hand when a former business associate was caught spreading rumors on the internet that I had stolen my own company's money and ran away. Obviously it was impossible for him to understand that someone could travel for an entire year without having committed a crime to obtain the funds.

Global nomads usually invent excuses for their travels such as charity, volunteering, learning languages, or writing books to eliminate the suspicions of vagrancy. The trend has been the same throughout history. It is acceptable to travel away from home, duties, and obligations in order to make money or work, conquer foreign lands, find artistic inspiration, or to grow spiritually. Consequently, these are the most commonly cited reasons for traveling.

Anthony's excuse is his NGO which allows him to dwell in the world. He has no other ties to his home country except his passport. As a Belgian, he cannot renew his travel document abroad so every time the book is filled up with visas and stamps, he has to travel back home. This occurs often for someone traveling as much as he does.

Regular visits to Belgium force Anthony to conform to the conventional concept of travel: it starts from home and it ends in the same place. However, Belgium is no longer home for Anthony. "I don't have a typical Belgian face so most of the time I don't feel at home because Belgians don't consider me at home either." Anthony comes from an immigrant family. His mother is Turkish, his grandmother was born in Cuba, and his father is from Italy.

Anthony considers himself stateless which makes many things easier: he can choose where he wants to be. Yet, it doesn't free him from the bureaucracy of travel. Although the universal declaration of human rights sublimely states that everyone has the right to leave any country, including one's own, in reality governments limit free movement in many ways: by passports, visas, residence permits and working permits. A price tag is also included as these documents are not available for free. According to the same logic, shouldn't there be a fee for freedom of religion and for freedom of speech as well?

For holidaymakers and business travelers passports and visas are rarely an obstacle. An American or European passport is enough in many South American and some African countries. Visas are required in Asia, but obtaining them is relatively easy if the travel time is less than one month. It is the longer stays that are anomalies in the eyes of the international visa system. States have difficulties in handling people who are not on a tourist trip, traveling for work, or immigrating with an expatriate spouse.

Global nomads have to find their way through legal loopholes or they have to pay bribes. Having visited all the countries in the world, Anthony is more than experienced in navigating the absurd system. He carries with him a packet of cigarettes although he doesn't smoke. That way he can always offer an inexpensive bribe to the border guards and avoid hours of waiting and humiliating interrogations.

Borders and airports are one of the most common places for legalized fraud and extortion. The heavily armed border guards can sometimes be stoned or drunk. Anthony told us about an incident that happened at an African border. The official told him and his travel companion that he was in a good mood and therefore the travelers could choose which one of their three travel bags was going to be his. Sometimes crossing the border by foot or by bicycle is forbidden so that local authorities get their share of the profits from taxi drivers, and in security checks the treatment can be too intimate: travelers must remove their shoes, raise their arms for inspection, or strip.

In addition to passports and visas, there are other inconveniences. Some countries require two-way flight tickets to make sure that the traveler will exit the country in time, while global nomads prefer to travel one way. In some Asian countries monthly visa-runs might be the only way to prolong tourist visas. Travelers are forced to exit and enter the country to get a new stamp and feed corruption.

Our Israeli nomad friend has experienced a multitude of problems that Americans and Europeans rarely encounter. When he lost his passport, he was suspected of selling it, and when he applied for a work permit to the United States, he had to list all American cities he had visited earlier and provide credit card bills for proof. The officials wanted to register everything that had happened during the previous ten years.

Despite the obvious problems visas and passports cause for travelers, one of our British nomads managed to find an upside to the visa system. Without due process, she would

just wander around and make no commitment to wherever
she is living. According to her, people would be lost in the
world without motivation, consideration and commitment.
"I've met a lot like that, and I'm one of them myself," she blurts.

Travel bureaucracy, however, is not innocent and without
consequences. Along with other official documents—credit
cards, various customer registers and medical records—it
mires us in a network which tracks our movements, financial
transactions, family relationships, and illnesses. Infomania is
explained by the best of citizens. The passport, for instance,
should vouchsafe the issuing state's guarantee of aid to the
traveler while in the jurisdiction of other states. In practice
the situation is different as embassies rarely have time, money
and interest to act.

There is another and far more important reason for gather-
ing of all the data. The state needs labor, taxes, soldiers and
citizens to maintain and increase its power. Thus it has to
determine who can be let out, when, and where. The state also
has to be able to locate and lay claim to its citizens who are
abroad. Those remaining beyond its reach form a danger as
they show the limits of the state's power. Rootlessness poses
a similar challenge. What to do with people, like Anthony,
who have lived in multiple countries and who feel alienated
from their country or origin? A stateless condition is not
recognized by any institution and no one can issue a passport
to a world citizen.

How has the world become so complicated? If traveling
and citizenship had been controlled in prehistoric times, the
world would not have seen the great migrations (300–700
BC) and the population would not have spread to such a wide
area as it now has. The need to control was born when forced
labor, in other words slavery and serfdom, were invented.
Slaves and serfs were considered property, and since they
could move around by themselves, owners had to find a way
to keep them from fleeing.

When serfdom declined, the state took over the task of

controlling the masses. The reasons were mostly economical and driven by fluctuations in the work market. Wage earners were allowed to move around more freely when the supply and the demand of labor were unbalanced. However, traveling always required an authorization. This document, which preceded the passport and identity papers, stated the official residence of the traveler. The practice suggested that it was abnormal to leave one's hometown. Without the right papers it was considered a crime.

During the Mercantile era, from the sixteenth century onwards, limitations were based on a belief which equated population with wealth and military power. The more citizens a state had, the wealthier and more powerful it was. Like slave owners, rulers disliked the idea of their property vanishing into thin air. They tried to keep an accurate account of their citizens and also keep a tight hold on them. An elaborate bureaucracy and technology were created in the process, and the same measures were also used for determining who deserved poor relief.

Until the triumph of capitalism and the nation-state in the nineteenth century, freedom of movement was restricted because of domestic catastrophes such as bad harvests, fear of emigration, unemployment, and the uncontrollable flux of beggars. It was after the French revolution that freedom of movement was guaranteed for the first time. Citizens got the right "to move about, to remain, [and] to leave." Passport controls were removed. This did not allow complete freedom as all emigrants living outside of France were suspected as possible traitors. Also the fear of wars, revolutions, foreign enemies, and spies made officials tighten the security measures.

As the examples from different centuries show, control of movement has existed since immemorial times and the methods have not changed much either. The most important issue is to recognize and distinguish the country's own citizens from aliens and track their movements. Tracking is based on paper documents as nationality cannot be read from people's appearance just like Anthony's case shows. Nationality is not an inherent but an arbitrary status.

Global nomads question the basis of the age-old system. An Argentinian nomad, who has spent more than half of his life out of his country, ponders why does the fact that he was born in Argentina make him Argentinian. What would happen if he went to Bhutan and strongly identified with the people and the country even though he was not born there? He recalls when a Japanese photographer took his picture. He was very happy at the time and he felt he belonged to Japan. Afterward people told him he looked Japanese. "We're a bit like chameleons, we change," he says.

When more and more people live in various countries during their lives, the system based on nationality and permanent residence is helplessly outdated. It might have worked in the old times when only a few people traveled or moved, but today people have several reference points and they form various relationships across state borders. Moreover, passports not only freeze physical but mental movement. People are not allowed to choose for themselves the kind of identity that states are not willing to validate. British travel writer Jan Morris, for instance, underwent a sex-change operation but was not able to travel as a woman before the British officials recognized his new sexual role.

The state has a monopoly on selling identity papers and traveling documents, but how many of us want to be property and merchandise of our state? Does freedom mean ubiquitous control and regulations? What if these regulations are created for our own good? Do the officials know better than we what is good for us?

I would give up my Finnish nationality if there were any viable options. I long for a country without any land or border, a virtual body, nomad land, or no man's land. Why should we divide the tiny earth into little fragments and call them countries, and then make all of them compete and fight with each other? We are all one, and we should be allowed to be one.

In the world of nation-states, it is unclear how such ideas might work. Still, cosmopolitanism offers important tools for questioning the supremacy of states by turning familiar concepts on their head. Do citizens exist for states or the other way round? Do people want the political systems to decide for them and intervene in their lives, or would they rather be left alone?

Various crises of the nation-state, such as financial crises, might increase the popularity of cosmopolitan ideas. At the same time cosmopolitanism has become more and more a capitalist project led by multinational corporations. It unites the elite while ordinary people continue to live in local communities. On a grassroots level, the idea of the world as one is nothing but a beautiful dream, but on a personal level it can exist if we stop respecting visas, passports, borders, and authorities.

The Great Escape

A mutual friend introduced us to forty-seven-year-old Frenchman Michel who calls himself "Nomad". Like Anick, he is a hyperactive member in hospitality exchange volunteering as a nomadic ambassador. When Michel started traveling, he didn't know about hospex yet but volunteered on the way. Then his seventy-four-year-old mother read a review about it and said to Michel, her voice full of irony: "Look at this Michel, with this service you can be homeless for the rest of your life." Michel joined right away.

Michel left France in 2007 when Nicholas Sarkozy was elected president because of his difference in political views. Michel joked to us about his plans to travel until 2012. Then he would vote for Sarkozy in the next election so that he could travel five more years.

Michel would gladly change his French nationality to world citizenship if such a thing was available. However, he is not fighting to abolish borders and visas as open-minded as it would be. "We are almost there," Michel acknowledges, "McDonald's is everywhere and diversity is killed like currencies in Europe."

Michel started traveling young. When he was fourteen, he joined the navy where he had an opportunity to sail around Africa. He didn't pursue his military career, however, but started doing odd jobs, mainly producing videos and managing websites, in various parts of France and in the French island of Martinique in the Caribbean.

Currently Michel earns his living by web hosting. He prefers to work as little as possible to be able to enjoy his freedom. His budget is twenty-one dollars a day: seven dollars for transportation, seven dollars for eating, and seven dollars for everything else such as entrance fees and doctors. In 2010 he had no budget for accommodation because he stayed with members of hospex.

Michel never liked running after money, but in France he was almost obliged to do it. Michel's answer was to quit. This, he notes, separates him from the housed. Too many people complain but they never do anything. Michel, on the hand, doesn't complain. He moves out.

Some people reproach Michel for fleeing conflicts and he readily admits, "Yes, I flee, because I don't like conflicts." Michel travels alone for the same reason: he doesn't want to fight. He knows he causes strong reactions in people and not everybody agrees with his opinions. Undiplomatic and without any taboos, he can be a tough cookie. Some people find him rude. Michel prefers shy boyfriends who follow him and let him make all the decisions. If he finds a suitable candidate and falls in love, he would like to travel together with his partner. The soft spot in his heart is that if he finds someone compatible, he doesn't want to dominate but lets the other person decide.

Michel's life philosophy is radical: "People play too easily with life. We need a license to drive, we need a license to go fishing, but for creating life we don't need any license. The most dangerous and stupid people can procreate." Michel believes that the earth would do fine without us. For him, the most green act would be to kill ourselves, and this, mind you, is not negative at all. Many think Michel's ideas are gloomy and pessimistic but he doesn't and I don't. He's just not afraid of death.

When we met Michel for the first time, he was touring Europe as a guest and stayed in other people's homes nine nights out of ten. Half a year later he had settled down in Penang, Malaysia, rented a condominium and started to host other travelers. He was going to host as many members as had accommodated him during his years of travels.

For Michel hospex is, bluntly put, a free bed. He knows that many members search for more sublime motives in the system, but for him accommodation is enough. If there happens to be cultural exchange as well, it's a plus but not a must. Hospitality exchange has given Michel two keys for traveling: accommodation and an interesting topic. He is not after sights. One magnificent cathedral is just one magnificent cathedral more. Instead, Michel prefers to meet people.

We stayed with Michel for one week and had the luxury of enjoying his overwhelming hospitality. All our travelers' needs were catered to. I was not even allowed to wash dishes and our host insisted on washing my dirty clothes. This prompted me to joke that Michel is the only global nomad I know who owns a washing machine.

When we left Michel's house, he was preparing to fly to France for a family visit. He showed us his long overcoat suited for French winter weather. It was Michel's flight coat as well because it had dozens of pockets. He could fit an enormous amount of stuff in the pockets, and as the clothes passengers are wearing are never weighed, Michel was able to avoid paying for excess luggage.

Radical Zen reformers in China and Japan came to my mind when I heard some of Michel's statements. Wandering was an important practice in Buddhism, too. It was Buddha himself who set the model. Having meditated under a holy fig tree, he experienced enlightenment and understood that all living is one and filled with nothing. Buddha wandered around teaching for forty years.

> *You cannot travel on the path until you have become*
> *the path itself.*
> —*Buddha*

Japan's Zen Buddhism is known for eccentric characters. One of them was monk Ikkyu (1394–1481) who wandered among bums, beggars, rogues, pirates, prostitutes, and wealthy merchants. This wild mob formed his street congregation. Ikkyu devoted himself to spiritual practice and didn't care for his appearance or social status. From time to time, he participated in the holy ceremonies in his village in a modest patched robe and straw sandals. When his rags became the object of interest, Ikkyu retorted, "Do not hold on to robes," and walked away.

Ikkyu wandered for almost thirty years. He declined offers to take a position as a Zen master or abbot in any temple. In his senior years, he settled down in a ramshackle house called "The Hut of the Blind Donkey." He lived simply and in poverty according to the ideals of the Japanese asceticism, *wabi-sabi*. Ikkyu's wandering Buddhism became known as Crazy Zen. He taught people, "how to shit and piss and just be ordinary."

Wandering was not a choice of a couple of eccentrics only. In the fourteenth century, the amount of wandering monks grew significantly because of political reasons. The shogunate was overthrown in an attempt to get the dethroned emperor back to power. The revolt was unsuccessful and led to an open conflict. It drove men from the Japanese court—poets, artists and army officers—to wander the road as monks in the same way that the election of Sarkozy drove Michel to wander.

During our years of travel, the most common question that has puzzled people is what did we escape from. Radical changes in lifestyle and leaving one's country are usually associated with shaking life experiences such as divorce, death of a close relative, or unemployment. Our adventure sprouted not from such dramatic incidents but rather from the dullness of everyday life. Päivi had been dreaming of traveling all her life, but she had only money to go abroad once a year or two when she was a student. At the time there were no easy escapes such as student exchange programs available. The few possibilities her university had to offer were reserved for students of philology and technological sciences.

After graduating and landing a well-paid job, Päivi had money but no more free time for traveling. She had high hopes about the types of stimulating challenges that work would offer her, and she assumed this would make her forget about traveling. However, she quickly grew tired of her career when she found out that no such challenges were to be found. Her answer was to start living for her annual four–six weeks of holidays which she spent roaming around Asia and South America.

I chose another path to the same end. The success of my company addicted me to work and made me a prominent open source software pioneer in Finland. By 2004, I had gained everything I had ever wanted but found myself unhappy. My life was more meaningless than ever. When I revised my company's values, a new value was added along with reliability, integrity and grit: happiness. I began to think about happiness in my own life and discovered that the company did not make me happy at all. I was simply fulfilling expectations of other people. This led me to abandon my company in the pursuit of love and happiness with Päivi.

Our love story combined the biggest passions of our lives. Päivi could travel with her loved one who provided her with the courage to leave the rat race, and I found the meaning of life without having to carry the dead weight of my possessions on my shoulders. I found someone to love and someone who loved me back.

Did we run away from our lives or did we run towards adventures? The negative motivations for traveling usually excite outsiders' imagination much more than the commonly accepted and positive ones. Some global nomads—knowing the audience's yearn for scandal—like to provoke. Our Spanish nomad got frustrated with Africans who failed to see the point of his bicycling around the world. They thought the government was paying him to cycle because otherwise he would have surely chosen to fly. The Spaniard replied, "On the contrary, I'm paying for the government—taxes."

Another provoker was one of the most celebrated Muslim wanderers, Moroccan Ibn Battuta (1304–1377), whose tremendous journey took him to the Middle East, the Asian steppes, India, China, and the sub-Saharan Africa. The trip totaled 75,000 miles (120,000 kilometers) and lasted almost thirty years. Ibn Battuta visited all Muslim countries. He always searched for new routes and refused to return to the same ones to which he had already traveled. Ibn Battuta endured many hardships during his travels and thus was a Romantic hero. He was robbed, kidnapped, shipwrecked, attacked by pirates, and he suffered from serious illnesses.

In the beginning, Ibn Battuta was not well-known among governors so he invited himself to the courts of sheiks and emirs. Later he became a celebrity who was summoned to speak about his adventures. His sense of his own importance grew and he often judged his hosts on their generosity. The leader of Mecca, he said, was a fine man, but those kings, who were stingy with their money and goods, didn't receive a good reference. Whenever Ibn Battuta felt that the gifts were entirely beneath him, he didn't hesitate to reject them.

Ibn Battuta was greedy for money, fame, and luxury to the extent that the sultan of Delhi reproached him for living beyond his means and running in debt. However, this showed only one side of the man who was full of contradictions. Ibn Battuta also dreamed of life as a monk, meditating and living simply. He was interested in Sufism, the mystical movement of Islam, and became a disciple of a famous Sufi Master. This whim lasted only five months as sultans, curiosity, and the pleasures of life dragged him back to the mundane world.

Was Ibn Battuta traveling for material or spiritual rewards?

Originally he had wanted to make a pilgrimage but his hunger grew on the way. Soon he wanted to travel the whole wide world. However, Ibn Battuta put these reasons into words only after returning to Morocco when the local sultan waited eagerly to hear his exciting stories. He sought to exaggerate and provoke.

Päivi believes Ibn Battuta was not only escaping from his country nor traveling after riches. He was plagued by restlessness which many global nomads also recognize in themselves from time to time. It can lead to obsessive traveling which guarantees well-being, or to a state of anxiety and meaninglessness, if the traveler is forced to stay put.

I am convinced that Päivi is one of those victims. I found the proof for my diagnosis when Päivi discovered that in the nineteenth century French doctors found a new disease called *dromomania*. It was classified as a form of mental illness.

Dromomaniacs were often in an unconscious state of mind and made strange and unexpected trips. One of the most famous dromomaniacs was the Frenchman Albert. Whenever he overheard a place name, he couldn't resist the call of the road. He was often surprised at where he had ended up. Most of the time he was broke doing odd jobs on the way or stealing, and sometimes the police arrested him but somehow he always managed to get back home. In fact, this is where dromomaniacs and global nomads differ from each other. Dromomaniacs had a home and a job—otherwise they couldn't have escaped.

Although dromomania is no longer identified as a disorder, stories associating long-term traveling and mental illness still remain. When a feature story about us was published in the monthly supplement of the biggest newspaper in Finland, the journalist who had written the story publicly talked about us with his colleagues on Facebook. They speculated that at least one of us had to be insane. We felt their comment wasn't fair as we insist we are both equally mad. This book provides the proof.

Life on the Road

AN ONLINE SEARCH FOR GLOBAL nomads was not as straightforward as we had hoped because travelers use different names for themselves. We found hobos, gypsies, vagabonds, female nomads, and frugal old farts to name but a few. In fact, it wouldn't have been easy to identify us as global nomads either. In the beginning we called ourselves escapees from the rat race and later full-time travelers, homeless loiterers, vagabond writers, and urban nomads.

Among the global nomads who have their own travel web site we found fifty-four-year-old American Andy who calls himself a hobo traveler. Unlike the American unemployed of the 1930s who traveled in box-cars, Andy flies. He adopted the name because he travels and works just like hobos did.

For Andy, traveling represents ultimate freedom: he can go wherever he pleases without any itinerary or plan. Andy doesn't know many people who would have the money, the ability, and the curiosity to live like he does. He was excited about the subject and reminded us that even the traditional nomads no longer move around. Mongolian *gers* are nowadays stationary. Andy feels he has the luxury that nobody else on the planet has: he can leave a culture and he can enter a culture. He knows the world on the street level unlike expatriates, and after spending a year or two in every continent except Antarctica, he has formed a unique global view.

Andy was born in Indiana. He has been touring the world for twelve years and he has no plans to stop. He admits being addicted. When we located Andy, he was in the Dominican Republic and only because he wanted to be there. If he doesn't like a place, he hops on a plane the next day. In fact, when Andy was in St. Martin in the Caribbean, he got up one morning and couldn't take it anymore. By one o'clock he was on the plane going to Guatemala. "I try not to enter countries when I'm in a bad mood," Andy joked.

Usually Andy enjoys a change of scenery at least every two months when he runs out of sights for photo shooting. Staying around longer would be living, not traveling. Andy appreciates drastic changes. If he has been in a Latin country speaking Spanish, he probably wants to go to an Asian or European country next.

Along with freedom, money is one of the most important things in traveling. Those who are not talking about money, are lying, Andy claims. Only retired people at a set income or people whose work is location independent can afford the nomadic lifestyle whereas young travelers in their twenties and thirties stop to work somewhere and hide it from others.

Back in the United States Andy worked as a real estate broker. He was good at marketing selling eighty houses a year, but he was also drinking a lot which caused him residual problems. Andy quit drinking twenty-three years ago and he doesn't go to bars anymore. He entertains himself by getting to know new cities and people, reading books and walking around in office supply stores. Andy loves gadgets. He is very mechanical and says he can fix anything but a broken heart.

During his travels, Andy has learned to create workarounds for everything he needs. He carries with him a clip-on light, an extension cord, and a little line for getting wrinkles out of his clothes. Wherever he goes, he builds himself a comfortable traveler's nest. It is composed of good internet, a hot shower in the room, some books to read, and some people to talk to.

Sometimes the quality of the nest makes it difficult to leave, but in the end Andy always chooses the road.

Andy's parents are proud of him. They worked in factories and dreamed of not having a boss. Andy is living their dream. He earns money with his travel website and although his income is very good, he also reminds us of the importance of making smart choices. In the Dominican Republic he lived in a ten-dollar room. The difference between a seventy-five-dollar room and Andy's room was nothing. "I'm just smart enough to take the ten dollar room," he says and gives a tip to those dreaming of traveling: learn to separate what you need and what you want. He adds, "What we need is friendship and food every day, and what we want is a new camera." Andy believes that anyone who can separate these two things can travel.

Andy's namesakes, hobos, started to roam around the United States in the late nineteenth century looking for work and traveling by freight trains. Some of them emphasized their gentlemanly behavior and willingness to earn their own living, while others bummed shamelessly.

Plunging into the world of hobos revealed that the gentlemanly and respectful side of their culture was romanticized when hobos were made heroes of popular films and books. In fiction, rugged men played harmonica, philosophized, and told stories as the freight trains happily clickety-clacked amidst breathtaking landscapes.

One of the most well-known hobo authors is Jack London (1876–1916) who was a patriot and a fierce critic of middle-class values. London's patriotism, however, faded away when he was arrested and sentenced to prison for thirty days for idle wandering on one of his hobo journeys. When the police asked him to give an account of his loitering, he was not able to name any hotel in town for his supposed lodging place—therefore he was labeled a vagrant as well. In court, London had no opportunity to defend himself as the verdict was given without hearing his side of the story. He never recovered from the shock that this intimate encounter with the American justice system caused him.

I don't believe in justice, but in absolute and unconditional forgiveness. Courts only offer people an opportunity for revenge and they protect the interests of the majority (read the power elite) at the expense of the minority. We are all one, and if we hurt someone else, we end up hurting ourselves. If we all agreed on this, the police, military and justice would become obsolete. Wouldn't it be better to love each other than punish and kill?

Although work was an integral part of hobos' lives, literary fiction spoke little of it. This was the case of London as well, both in his books and in his own life: he would rather beg than condescend to work. As a result, it seemed that hobos were on an eternal job-seeking mission without ever finding any, or maybe not even having a real motivation for bread-winning. If they had found a job, it would have been the end of the excitement. The plausible excuse for stealing rides would have vanished.

Another reason for ignoring hobos' work was the casual jobs they did. Many helped in menial farm work such as harvesting crops which didn't provide myth-makers with thrilling material. Hobos preferred to brag about their wanderings instead. Nor did movies and books tell anything about the grim social and economic conditions that produced the hobo. Thus hobo became merely an enchanting rogue who hopped box-cars for sport. This interpretation of hobo culture still persists.

Neither Paivi, Andy or I have tried hoboing Our only bumming experiences have been on French trains where conductors are often too lazy to sell tickets. Nevertheless, there are many similarities between hobos and global nomads. Hobos tried to get by with as little as possible to keep their freedom from middle-class shackles such as work, house, and money. In a similar manner some global nomads question economic growth, ideals of the consumer society, and the middle-class work ethic. They search for the meaning of life free from conventional restrictions and safety nets.

How do global nomads finance their travels and how much does traveling life cost? Only a few are millionaires, but money is not an issue for most as they have learned to live with little. Yoga teacher Phoenix has always just decided what he wants to do and then he does it. Money has been nothing that he has ever considered as a deciding factor. For him, money is just an excuse people use for not doing what they say they want to do.

As most global nomads don't have a house, car or other running costs in their country of origin, their costs depend solely on their daily consumption. Unlike tourists, they seek affordable ways of traveling and take time in acquiring cheap tickets. Haste always increase costs while flexibility saves money.

Our lifestyle has changed completely since leaving Finland. We worked in business where image is everything, and as a result working became one of our biggest costs. By working we exchanged our time for money. After the trade, we had less time but more money, and so we patched our reduced free time by buying time-saving products and services such as home electronics and cleaning services. In addition expensive clothes, shoes, and cars were needed to keep up our image. As the amount of needs caused by work increased all the time, our costs grew exponentially.

Nowadays we do all the housework by ourselves and we take pleasure in wandering in supermarkets comparing prices and finding the best bargains. Our food costs are lower than ever not only because of the more reasonable cost levels of the countries we have been visiting, but mostly because we prefer seasonal and local products. It is possible to spend a lot of money buying Western food products in countries where they are not produced and commonly consumed. For instance dairy products are expensive in China where most of the population suffers from genetic lactose intolerance, and alcohol is expensive in Muslim countries where religion forbids drinking. Sniffing cocaine, on the other hand, is expensive everywhere.

Our clothing budget is minimal as we usually wear shorts and T-shirts, most of which we have received from other people. If we were ever invited to a formal dinner, we would have to decline the friendly offer because of our modest outfits.

Our current costs are way below the Western subsistence levels. The following statistics show all our travel costs from November 2006 until February 2011. All sums have been converted to US dollars and they include everything: travel costs, food, rent, hotel nights, clothes, health care, and working costs (laptops, cameras, and the costs of writing books and making films).

Our monthly living costs

Thailand	11/2006	$ $ $ $ $ $ $ $
	12/2006	$ $ $
Cambodia	1/2007	$ $ $ $
	2/2007	$ $ $ $ $
	3/2007	$ $ $ $ $
	4/2007	$ $
	5/2007	$ $
	6/2007	$ $
	7/2007	$ $
Vietnam	8/2007	$ $ $
Mongolia	9/2007	$ $
China	10/2007	$ $ $
	11/2007	$ $ $
	12/2007	$ $ $
Hong Kong	1/2008	$ $ $ $ $

Our monthly living costs

	2/2008	$ $ $ $ $
	3/2008	$ $ $ $
France	4/2008	$
	5/2008	$ $ $
	6/2008	$ $ $
	7/2008	$ $ $
	8/2008	$ $ $
	9/2008	$ $
Spain	10/2008	$ $ $ $ $ $ $ $ $ $ $ $ $ $ $ $
France	11/2008	$ $ $ $ $ $
	12/2008	$ $
	1/2009	$ $ $
	2/2009	$ $
	3/2009	$ $ $
	4/2009	$ $
	5/2009	$ $
	6/2009	$ $ $
	7/2009	$ $ $
	8/2009	$ $ $
	9/2009	$ $ $
Italy	10/2009	$ $ $
	11/2009	$ $ $
	12/2009	$ $
	1/2010	$ $ $ $ $ $ $
	2/2010	$
	3/2010	$ $ $
	4/2010	$ $

Our monthly living costs

	5/2010	$ $
	6/2010	$ $ $ $
	7/2010	$ $ $
	8/2010	$ $ $ $
	9/2010	$ $
	10/2010	$ $ $
Greece	11/2010	$ $ $ $ $ $ $ $ $
Kenya	12/2010	$ $ $
Tanzania	1/2011	$ $ $ $ $ $ $ $ $ $ $ $ $
Malaysia	2/2011	$ $ $

$ ≈ 250 dollars. Our total monthly costs have varied between 213–3,352 dollars with the average of 750 dollars a month.

Our average spending for the fifty-two months was 752 dollars for the two of us (376 dollars per person), varying between 213 dollars and 3,352 dollars per month. The reason for the cost peak in October 2008 was not expensive Spain. We were robbed in Alicante bus station and lost a backpack containing a hefty wad of cash and a laptop.

Our cost of living has not varied much between countries and continents. The reverse growth trend can be explained with changes in our consumption habits. In Thailand we drank wine and Irish coffee and ate animal products; in Cambodia we became vegetarians and stopped drinking; in Italy we became vegans. The new diet has made eating in restaurants impossible in many places which has lowered our living costs even further. Instead of taxis and renting cars, we prefer to walk, and accommodation is cheaper thanks to renting and using hospitality exchange. At the end of the day, costs depend greatly on bargaining skills, cleverness and a willingness to be comfortable with less. Waiting and negotiating are always profitable as time and patience tend to lower prices. The biggest single costs that remain are laptops, cameras, and intercontinental airline tickets.

The less I consume, the happier I am. My consumption is now in better balance with the resources of the earth, and as I consume less, I also pollute less. However, I'm still far from low consumption. Over a billion people—one in five—get by with less than a dollar per day. Compared to that the hundred million poor in the Western countries are extremely wealthy. They are poor merely because they cannot consume enough to keep national economies growing.

I believe that poverty exists only because there are rich people. Someone is poor only if someone else has got more. If we really want to eradicate poverty, we have to first deal with the rich. While it is not possible to persuade others to do that, everyone of us can make the decision in their own life and get rid of their possessions.

How do global nomads earn their living? Most of them work regularly or temporarily, or they live on their savings. Exploiting social security is not possible as countries are not keen to offer benefits for people who spend their time and money abroad. Using loopholes in the system might not be worth the trouble in the long run.

Those who consider the nomadic lifestyle as a temporary phase in life, have usually saved for their trip. They have a budget and when the money runs out, they return back to work. French hitchhiker Ludovic spent 35,000 dollars during his five-year tour. He slept anywhere and didn't need any money for transportation. Most of his budget went to food, internet and clothes. In addition to savings, he gave lectures on the way and had a couple of sponsors.

The majority of those traveling without a time limit work either regularly or when they have to. Most common jobs are in IT: web page design, maintenance and programming, or selling ads to travel websites like hobo Andy. Location doesn't matter as long as there is an internet connection available.

Writing and translating are location independent. We

work periodically four–five months a year and then idle the
rest of the time. This doesn't apply to this book, however, as
the subject immersed us totally for a couple of years and it
seems that we will continue with it in the future as well. Our
money comes mostly from grants. The Finnish-language book
market is so small, only five million people, that writers are
subsidized. With our current cost levels and the ever-lowering
trend our modest income has been more than enough.

Some global nomads write to local newspapers and magazines about their travels and destinations, and for the English
speakers teaching English is the most common way to make
money abroad. Most of the time no diplomas are needed;
being a native speaker is enough.

Others support themselves with portable work such as
massage and making jewelry. Phoenix teaches yoga, ayurvedic
medicine, and meditation, and he is also a massage therapist.
He considers himself lucky. Although he has never had much
money, it has always been enough for all he has needed. He
lived in India for a year on a few thousand dollars and when
he was hiking in Spain in the route of El Camino de Santiago
he spent almost no money at all as all he bought was red wine.

The type of work matters for those global nomads who
want to express themselves and their values through work.
They make no distinction between work and leisure as both
are integral parts of their lifestyle. However, this is not the
case for all. Like hobos, some global nomads readily take
odd jobs to get money for traveling and then travel until the
money runs out. They rarely save or invest their earnings
except maybe for accumulating a buffer to tide them over
between jobs. If the buffer is enough, global nomads will
forgo earning opportunities.

The global nomads we know have been working in construction sites and restaurants, as photo models, assistant
actors in Bollywood, as guides, cooks, and bus drivers. They
have become jacks of all trades, and as long as they believe
in their own charisma, searching for a job abroad is never

difficult. Cyclists and hitchhikers might also have sponsors who provide them with gear. In return, global nomads advertise their sponsor in their blogs.

Those global nomads who do not work anymore, live on their savings that were earned through stints in the midst of traveling or before adopting the nomadic lifestyle. For most, the secret of extended traveling lies in low costs rather than in high income. Global nomads have minimized consumption and see buying merely as an addiction with which people patch holes in their lives or define their identity. Already Aristotle made the important distinction between needs and wants that hobo Andy talked about.

Andy resents consumerism in the United States. When people define themselves by what they buy, they become enslaved. Yet, Andy is proud of his heritage. For him, the value of being an American is that he doesn't know how to give up. Every American truly believes they can be the president of the United States and the leader of a free world. Andy is grateful that nobody put any limit in his head. He can do anything.

Do I love Americans, Andy ponders and reckons that his relationship to his compatriots is ambiguous. Americans can be demanding because they don't have to live with anything. They know they can change the world. People often say to Andy that he should "live with it," but for him it is difficult. He still believes he can make the world a better place.

The high price Americans pay for their dream is something Andy dislikes. Americans work from twelve to sixteen hours a day. When Andy calls friends up, they ask if they can call back. "They don't realize they are so obsessed with their desire to be somebody that they forget they really are nobody. They are just somebody wanting to be somebody else," Andy says.

Like Andy, most American nomads are proud of their country, but we also met one who feels so alienated from the United States that he doesn't want to have anything to do with Americans. He considers the lack of alternatives as one of the greatest problems of nationality. One's nationality cannot be chosen neither can it be rejected unless it is tediously exchanged for another nationality. Nations are obligatory communities which in most cases can only be entered by birth and exited by death. Another American nomad ponders that patriotic world views have had a bad impact on our planet. The powers that are in control don't recognize boundaries, but they want to convince us that we should be patriotic toward our country because it keeps people separate.

Patriotism creates xenophobia. I too resent the fear of the other which is ever more present in Finland today. Finnish culture is fairly homogeneous and Finns are not used to seeing people who look different and who have a different way of life. Having lived my childhood in the Finland of the 1970s, my encounters with foreigners were rare. Getting to know people from other cultures was not encouraged, and there was no natural way to make any contact. The true Finn mentality, which has again gained support because of globalization and EU integration, was prevailing: Finland was for Finns only and no foreigners were welcome.

When I was in school in the '70s, I often heard the mantra, "It is like winning the lottery to be born in Finland." It was a time of protectionism and flag-waving politicians. Everyone was suppose to favor domestic products, the ones with the blue-and-white flag on them, no matter how unhealthy or bad they were. When I later thought I had finally got rid of the patriotic pathos, my mother reminded me of my proud heritage by saying that she doesn't have to travel anywhere because everything is so much better in Finland. Needless to say, I haven't seen my parents or siblings since our visit in Finland in 2006 as they are not willing to travel abroad.

Criticizing, though rightly, a country and culture is often perceived as arrogant and malicious because people take the critique personally. My criticism toward Finland, or more generally towards each and every country in the world, has been met with much opposition and it has cost me some friendships. Although Finland is considered to be one of the vanguards of freedom of speech, assessment of this freedom fails to take into account peer pressure. By criticizing I have excluded myself from society.

Like charity entrepreneur Anthony, I often celebrate the positive meaning of rootlessness: it makes me free to choose. I also love to describe myself as unemployed and homeless, but so prevailing are the negative meanings of these words that people are almost without exception on the defense: "You're not unemployed. You write books!" a friend of ours opposed. "You're not homeless," Canadian hitchhiker Anick exclaimed, "You have so many places and houses to live in."

There is also another meaning and interpretation I have not been able to shake off despite my efforts: for others, I will always be a Finn. National stereotypes follow me with my passport everywhere I go, but fortunately there is one good thing about Finland: usually nobody has ever heard of it.

Where do you come from?
Finland.
Oh, England? Yes, I know England. A very good
country, rich and green.

Freedom

After getting in touch with the first global nomads, our task became easier as they all gave us new leads. We are especially grateful to American author Rita Golden Gelman. After writing the book *Tales of a Female Nomad* (2001), she had been collecting contacts in order to gather a group of nomads for *The Oprah Show*. Although the project never realized, her network was intact and at our disposal.

Forty-three-year-old American Suzan was among the global nomads we found from Rita's network. Suzan had contacted Rita after reading her book. As a freelance journalist, Suzan had written about her nomadic lifestyle and travel destinations for various magazines, and she had also considered writing a book. The time was not right, however, as Suzan was occupied with other projects.

Suzan began globetrotting after losing her job. She had been working in a record company as the head of media relations, but as the music business began to slow down at the beginning of the new Millennium, the record label folded and Suzan was suddenly out of work.

Losing her job was a huge shock to Suzan who was a

workaholic and didn't know what to do with all her free time. She couldn't get another job because she was considered overqualified. The companies didn't want to pay her a high salary but instead hired the younger colleagues she had trained. Suzan was just over forty but already considered outside the hectic work market.

After a year of being bitter and depressed, and another year freelancing and struggling to make her mortgage, Suzan decided that she was not going to beg for work anymore. She was single and free to do anything she wanted, and as she had always had wanderlust, the decision was easy. She sold everything—her house, her car, her furniture, her clothes, and two hundred pairs of shoes—packed her backpack and left.

Suzan traveled for a year and returned to the United States for a couple of months. People she ran into asked where she had been, but she realized that they were not really interested about her travels but what she was working on. "Hollywood is all about what people are doing, what celebrities they are involved with, and how can they help others because that equates their status," Suzan explains. She realized she didn't want to be there anymore and went traveling again. She had already had more than her share of entertainment business.

Suzan had started her career in public relations in the legendary Mudd Club in New York in the early 1980s. She cavorted with and interviewed many of the era's notable punk and new wave artists. She also got involved in cocaine, which in those days was not considered addictive. It was socially acceptable. When Suzan got a job in a high profile public relations firm and started doing music PR, along came drinking. Suzan worked for many famous people and moved to Los Angeles. She toured with Scorpions and worked with George Michael, Simply Red, and Run DMC.

"It was a wild and crazy time. Limos, helicopters, backstage parties—basically all the excesses and perks that defined the 80s," Suzan reminisces. It usually takes time before she reveals having worked with famous people as it is not relevant to her anymore. Rather, it puts her in a different category. Suzan believes that in the end we are all on the same playing field.

After working for others, Suzan founded her own PR company from where she was headhunted to the record company where her career in music business finished. It wasn't the end of the world after all, although Suzan had feared it. Instead, another door opened. Suzan discovered her latent artistic flair and started to make jewelry and hand-painted clothing. Of these, jewelry became her main business. Suzan has now established her own collection which she sells all over the world, on beaches and street corners. When we found her, she was in Costa Rica where business was good.

Suzan has come to believe that there are no accidents, just a series of circuitous events. Losing her job was the beginning of an entirely new and exciting chapter in her life. She has learned, especially from younger travelers and gypsies, that options are so much broader than she ever dared to think. She adopted a philosophy of keeping her heart, mind, and options open.

So far Suzan's nomadic journey has taken her from the Amazon to the Ganges, from Mount Sinai to Mount Everest on six continents. She has provided tsunami aid in South India, worked with a rural school in Nepal and with a Tibetan Woman's group in Dharamsala, lived with the Bedouins in Jordan and with a former sadhu in India, studied reiki, tai chi, yoga, ayurvedic massage, and metaphysics.

Suzan describes the intensity of her travel experiences using the wow-factor. If she is in a place that is alien to her point of reference or completely new culturally, she says, "Wow!" She feels like she is alive and learning. When the wow-effects fade, Suzan changes scenery and looks for something new. Leaving is easy as she is not tied to places, long leases, property-owning, and tight social relationships. "Sometimes I think I have too much freedom because I have a difficult time making decisions where to go next," she says laughing.

Most often Suzan follows her gut. When she was in Israel,

a friend of hers put an Atlas in front of her. Suzan decided to go to Morocco but she couldn't find a reasonable flight so she flew to Spain planning to take a boat from there to Morocco. In Spain, however, Suzan was contacted by a couple of friends from India who were living in Italy, and soon she found herself living in a squat in Pisa.

Like Suzan, we have been zigzagging the globe randomly taking pleasure in changing the continent once in a while. We have only one plan: no plans. From an outsider's point of view our route probably looks like a fur ball without a head or tail, but ready-made schedules and plans are merely a nuisance on the road as they change for various reasons that are out of our control. Like when we crossed the border from Brazil to Santa Cruz in Bolivia, the estimated travel time was eighteen hours. Our transport which resembled an old army truck rather than a bus, drove through thick jungles and river bottoms. As a result, the tires blew three times and the whole trip took twenty-eight hours. We ran out of food, our stomachs were complaining loudly, and we had not a single Bolivian peso in our pockets. On one of the many coffee and lunch breaks, a little Bolivian girl gave us a big loaf of freshly baked bread and saved us from starvation. We will never forget her friendly gesture.

The longer we have traveled, the slower we go. Little by little we have learned to give up the Western concept of time, and we no longer feel the need to fill up empty moments. When our stress eased up, the focus of the journey has shifted from the future into the present moment which has made us happy. After all, happiness can only be found in this very moment, here and now.

When I was working, the will to get more money and more possessions always shifted my attention to the future. Junk seemed to guarantee a better, wealthier, and more secure future, but in reality I was only delaying the fulfillment of my needs. I never questioned what was truly better. Did better really mean higher salary, more shares, a bigger house, and a bigger car, or in general, more purchasing power? Now my definition of better includes: I carry less things in my backpack, I travel slowly with no particular destination in mind, and I consume as little as possible. If I'm lucky there is a beach and a mountain nearby for long walks, hikes, and swimming. Sometimes better might mean leaving the easy life behind and going to dangerous places or rough conditions.

I often ask people what would they do if they knew they were going to die tomorrow. How would they continue living if every day they were granted just one day more, day by day, in a complete uncertainty? The question shifts the focus from the future to the present moment and in the process the journey itself becomes more important than the destination. As the old proverb states: "It's not the destination but the journey that fulfills us." I dwell in motion.

Päivi suggests that the word *wandering* describes nomadic travels better than traveling. Its origin is in Latin *vagari* which means to 'wander', 'roam', 'be unsettled', 'spread abroad'. At least the word describes perfectly our own aimless roamings. Wandering has also negative connotations. It can refer to wandering thoughts or a wandering mind, lack of concentration, absent-mindedness. It can mean being lost, lost in one's thought or physically lost in an unknown place. Wandering is also used to describe Alzheimer's disease. The patient suffers from a memory loss and starts to wander with dangerous consequences. He might get lost, fall, and break his bones.

For global nomads, wandering means a lack of a rigid plan and freedom to do whatever they please. Their lifestyle is extreme, as one of the pioneers of tourism research, Erik Cohen, stated when he heard about our book project. Cohen discovered and wrote about the predecessor of global nomads, the drifter. Drifters were self-reliant individuals who—in order to preserve the freshness and spontaneity of their travel experience—traveled without an itinerary, timetable, destination, and well-defined purpose much in the same way as global nomads. Since the publication of Cohen's article in

1973, drifters have rarely been the subject of research, simply because they have been too difficult to reach.

After noticing the many similarities between drifters and global nomads, we traveled to Bangkok to meet Cohen personally. At the end of a short discussion in a coffeehouse, Erik invited us to his home in the Bangkok suburbs. The evening was memorable. We bought groceries for dinner from the local market, and then Erik took us for a speed walk. We had a hard time keeping pace with him although he was already seventy-nine. Erik and his wife kindly let us borrow their kitchen and we prepared dinner which was a welcome break from our typical guesthouse diet consisting of toast, instant noodles, and fruits.

Later in the evening we heard the story of how the idea of the drifter had occurred to Erik. He had been living in Ayacucho, a town in the central Andes of Peru, when a German approached him on the street and asked to lodge in his apartment for a day or two. The man was a chemistry student who had arrived in the central Peruvian Sierra from the Atlantic coast of Brazil via the Amazon River. He had been traveling alone in a small boat curing himself of the tropical illnesses he suffered from in the wilderness. His trip took about seven months during which he was sometimes alone for such a long time that he had started to talk to himself. The German man, the forefather of global nomads, had many similarities with our Ferrari repairman in Kuala Lumpur. Päivi was excited about the possibility to continue Erik's research.

Most global nomads are unaware of other global nomads. Often the whole lifestyle initiates from a whim. Hobo Andy went to Mexico for what he thought would be a six-week vacation from his job but he was soon hooked. Having got used to nomadic freedom, even the smallest musts became repulsive to him. Andy resents forced social relationships which are based on repetition. The repetition is what most people need, but Andy doesn't. He doesn't need to hear the same opinion every week, nor the same person complaining about the same problem every week.

For us a similar must was owning a mobile phone. In the beginning we dutifully carried one with us as we had received it as a wedding present. When our mobile was stolen in Bali, Indonesia, we were at first sorry for loosing the precious gift, but later we noticed how relaxing life was without it. We didn't have to remember to charge the battery, argue whose turn it was to silence the polyphonic nuisance, or worry about it getting lost.

Freedom can only be understood once it has been experienced. In Finland, the mobile phone represented freedom for us. We were able to go anywhere and still be available. Later we discovered that this thought was a mere defense mechanism. Life would have become intolerable if we had perceived phones as enslaving as we now view them to be.

Western countries revere freedom, but how often people are only convincing themselves that the musts in their life are their own choices just like we did? Society is like an aquarium: it looks spacious as long as you don't hit the glass.

Freedom and the amount of choices available are always relative. The point of reference is made up of our own and other peoples' attachments. Although this comparison makes freedom understandable, it also has a negative effect: it creates oppositions.

Oppositions play a major role in the stories with which people tell about themselves, others, and the world. In the nomadic thought, the prevailing opposition is between the nomad and the sedentary, or more commonly known as the couch potato. Its roots can be traced to the story of Cain and Abel in the Bible. Abel was a shepherd of flocks, the first nomad; Cain a farmer and the founder of the first city. When both brothers gave an offering to God, only Abel's offering was regarded which infuriated Cain. He attacked his brother and killed him. God punished Cain by condemning him to wander restlessly on the earth for the rest of his life.

According to the story, wandering is a curse, and it is

precisely this outcast image that has attracted bohemians, artists and adventurers to live on the road and mythologize their experiences. Global nomads, however, rather even out the difference between the two. Yoga teacher Phoenix likes both. He likes the feeling of stability when he can wake up in the morning and everything is the same. It offers him a wonderful sense of peace and security. But when he is on the road, he is excited because he never knows where he is going to sleep and where he is going to wake up.

Most global nomads like to encourage others to travel thus lowering the threshold between the sedentary and the nomadic lifestyle. French nomad Michel always says to his admirers that they can do the same in ten minutes if they want to. While traveling and living abroad used to be privileges of the elite, lower transportation costs have brought them to within everyone's reach. Now, it is a matter of choice.

The role of the encourager is not always grateful. Twenty-nine-year-old Portuguese Ciro, who has been on the road since 2007, admits that his passion for traveling is not shared with many Portuguese. Reviving the legacy of his ancestors, the great Portuguese explorers was, in fact, one of the reasons that motivated and thrilled him. Ciro blames close family ties and financial reasons for the death of the tradition. People have to work and they have to have a family. They prefer to spend the year working and travel for a couple of weeks on their holiday.

Whereas work and money drove the great explorers to the seas in the old days, now they are keeping the Portuguese—and in general most people—at home. Has traveling lost the prestige it used to have? Is it considered a mere waste of time when one could horde possessions instead?

This is the prevailing attitude at least in Finland. I have read in the news about the dangers young people expose themselves to when making a gap year abroad, when they could study in a university and get a degree. Recently an influential Finnish bankster proposed that free time should be taxed so that people would have less incentive to prefer their own time over work. Perhaps the next innovation would be to fine people for an excessive night sleep.

I gave up my attempts to inspire others after realizing that I was time and again caught in a yes-but game. When I tried to invent various ways in which my discussion partner could realize his dreams, he turned all my proposals down one after another with sentences beginning "Yes, but."

> *Homeowner: I wish I could travel. It would be like*
> *living a dream.*
> *Me: Why don't you start traveling?*
> *Homeowner: I have been thinking about it, yes, but we*
> *just moved to a new house and now I have to pay the*
> *mortgage.*
> *Me: If you sell the house, you can get money to pay*
> *back the loan and travel. Life on the road is much*
> *cheaper.*
> *Homeowner: Yes, it probably is, but my wife and*
> *children don't agree. Friends are very important for*
> *children not to mention a familiar and safe environ-*
> *ment. Having a family makes one conservative.*

The game continued until I ran out of options. Then the homeowner was able to free himself from guilt of not doing anything by saying: "Didn't I tell you. I can't do it."

The conversation can be interpreted in various ways. It can be complimentary: the homeowner expresses his admiration for the global nomad's lifestyle by saying he would like to do the same. In reality, he has no interest to go anywhere. He is happy with his life and the discussion is meaningless small talk. Another option is that traveling for him is a pipe dream. Dreaming about it is enough, or he is too afraid of the consequences to leave. Leaving would also make his dreams come true, and thus his riskless exit from dull everyday life would be lost.

Sometimes the homeowner might genuinely be interested

in changing his lifestyle but he is not ready to take the step yet. Motivation has to be strong so that immobilizing factors will be overcome. If one surrenders to fears, dreams will be buried until some shaking life experience such as divorce, bankruptcy, or serious illness resurrects them again. At that time, it might be too late to leave.

Instead of participating in the fruitless yes-but game, we can always choose to believe the mantra: "When you really want something, it's not hard." In the end, all depends on ourselves and what we are willing to make of our lives. If we really want to, we all can be free as a global nomad.

School of Life

We were visiting an American expatriate woman as guests of hospitality exchange in Nanjing, China. After telling her about our nomadic journey, she got excited and told us she had just been hosting a French nomad who was on a round-the-world hitchhiking tour. The Frenchman had left a few weeks earlier and was headed to Tibet. We managed to locate him in the French Riviera after he had concluded his tour.

Thirty-two-year-old Ludovic thumbed his way round the world in five years. He started in January 2003 and visited North-Korea and the Antarctic to name just a few of the highlights of his journey. Ludovic's adventures were varied. On his way to Tibet, he was hiding from the Chinese policemen in trucks; while crossing the Atlantic he stowed away on boats where he peeled potatoes for the crew.

Ludovic considers his journey a fantastic school of life. Although business school taught him many things, it didn't teach him anything about the world's wonders and miseries. The French population represents only one percent of the world population, and Ludovic wanted to learn how the other ninety-nine percent lived.

Hitchhiking enabled Ludovic to be in constant contact with local people. He was already a seasoned traveler before the journey. He had started hitchhiking when he was sixteen from his father's suggestion. Ludovic's overly protective mother had taken him everywhere, but his father told her to stop. The boy had to learn how to stand on his own, and for this he needed to be more independent and resourceful.

Ludovic started hitchhiking first around his city, then he expanded his territory gradually to the region, France, and Europe. The more Ludovic traveled, the more he wanted to see, and soon he was planning a round-the-world tour. He had had an easy life and he wanted to challenge himself. He adopted a motto: "Life is not a restaurant but a buffet. Stand up and help yourself."

Ludovic left his first job at Price Waterhouse Coopers, where he had worked as a consultant. Many of his colleagues and friends thought he was crazy. Why would he sleep on the floor and on the streets when he could have a nice job and a comfortable life? On the other hand, there were those who understood his wish to test himself and they pushed him to follow his dreams.

The journey was originally supposed to take two years but plans changed along the way. Two years wasn't enough, but after five years Ludovic was already tired. He felt in harmony with himself and he was ready to do other things. He went back to France. After seeing sixty countries, he still believes it is a good country to live in. Home country is an integral part of Ludovic's identity, although he also regards himself as a world citizen. He looks at everyone as brothers and sisters regardless of religion or country.

If Ludovic had a dream for the humanity, it would be a world without borders where visa stickers and passports would be on display in museums for future generations to laugh at. He regards the current system as absurd. "I may have toured the world, but many times I had the impression that I went to the moon. When we look at the world from the moon, we look at things differently and we realize there are no borders."

Patience and persistence are just two of the things Ludovic has learned from hitchhiking. During his journey Ludovic received 1,300 rides and watched 20,000 cars rush by. He waited for lifts and border crossings a total of 10,000 hours. The longest continuous waiting time was twenty-eight hours. The slow pace gave Ludovic an opportunity to step back from his busy life and think. It was an awakening experience which changed his perception of time and what is really important in life. After seeing so much suffering, Ludovic started to appreciate life more and he became aware how fortunate he was to come from little Europe. He also learned to appreciate little pleasures of life, such as a bed and toilet paper, which he had taken for granted in the past. Ludovic also became ecologically conscious. He learned to see the consequences of his actions and he understood how fragile the world is in terms of water and energy access and biodiversity conservation.

Traveling does offer a great opportunity for learning. Päivi told me that this was already the view of French philosopher Jean-Jacques Rousseau (1712–1778) who gave a series of instructions how to make a successful tour. One of the most important goals he set for traveling was to open the journeyman's mind. Although commerce and arts also blended peoples, they prevented them from studying one another. As the journeys were made with utilitarian purposes on mind, there was no further incentive to continue the interaction once the profits of the other nations were reaped. Rousseau considered this as a form of cannibalism.

For Rousseau, traveling was a rite of passage that made young men full-blooded members of society. The journey's most risky event was leaving one's home which required denial of the father—although only temporarily, because homecoming strengthened the bond between father and son. Sigmund Freud later added that journey always involved a feeling of guilt, because by traveling further than the father, the son criticized him.

The nomadic lifestyle is often interpreted as a statement that criticizes home and home country. In my case, the fears related to traveling manifested themselves in superstitious horror images that my friends painted before me: by leaving society and uprooting myself I would suffer an irrefutable loss and drive myself to exile.

Traveling was a tricky business, Rousseau admitted. It radically changed the traveler. Those who returned home, were irreversibly changed for the rest of their lives. More men came back wicked than good, Rousseau believed, because they were more inclined to evil than to good. The few lucky ones, whose good nature had been refined, returned better and wiser than they had left.

Rousseau's expections were surpassed by his top student Émile. He adapted to various countries and circumstances so well that he felt at home everywhere, thus becoming his own home. The same applies to global nomads, although one critical difference remains. Émile literally returned home which was the highlight of his journey. Rousseau believed that the profits of journeying only realized themselves upon returning. Traveling had no value in itself.

With his strict guidelines, Rousseau seems to have wanted to keep amateurs away from the road. According to him, in the happy times of antiquity, ordinary people neither traveled nor engaged in philosophy leaving both tasks to professionals. Rousseau himself spent various periods of his life as a vagabond. He went on foot, played the beggar, and launched pedestrianism as a trendy pastime for the intellectual elite.

One of the legacies of the educational tour still persists: travelers have the habit of summing the lessons learned. Jewelry seller Suzan believes she has become more openminded, experienced and humble thanks to her travels. She is grateful for what she has and she can live with a lot less than before. For yoga teacher Phoenix, traveling has taught him that everything he needs is inside. He is happier with a backpack on his back than in a house full of junk.

Asceticism is a natural consequence of travel, just like it was for spiritual wanderers of old. Monks carried only a few items with them and lived without creature comforts. In a similar way, global nomads view possessions as a mere burden that enslave their owners and tie them down. For me, one of the most liberating experiences was getting rid of all the things I had gathered over the years. I had bought them in hope of making my life comfortable, but in vain. I kept longing for something else and Päivi kept longing for being elsewhere. The junk failed to make us happy and it failed to bring us a feeling of security. On the contrary, I had more worries because of my accumulated possessions. No matter how hard I tried, the possibility of a loss always remained. Like the English upper class in the sixteenth century, I was staggered by the thin line that distinguishes the rich from the poor. A stock market crash or a bank crisis could ruin all my efforts in a single day.

Was worrying worth it? Did it make me happy? Obviously not. This realization made it easy for me to leave everything behind, even when most people around me warned against it.

Traveling also teaches global nomads to critically assess their immaterial legacy. Seeing other cultures and lifestyles produces an alienating effect which can help to question the models and values learned at home. But just how people transform their ideals is a drastic and a rather little-known process. Studies don't tell us much about how it is actually accomplished.

From our experience we have noticed that getting rid of ideals learned in early childhood is hard. Our curse is punctuality. If we need to be somewhere at a particular time, we will go there well in advance to be sure that we won't be late. If there are delays and we cannot keep our promises, we get stressed. We have tried to be more carefree, but in vain. Instead, we have adopted another strategy: we avoid agreeing on appointments, making plans or promises.

I also work for another goal: I would like to get rid of my ability to read. I feel that I was irreversibly damaged and violated by the Finnish school system. They knew better than me what I needed in life, and now I am paying for their patronizing. The easiest solution to this vexing problem has been to travel in countries that use characters other than the Latin alphabet. For instance in China, I wasn't able to read roadside advertisements and other meaningless texts before even noticing what had happened.

When we were touring around the country of China, the consequences of illiteracy were many. In railway stations we tried to spot English-speaking Chinese to help us buy tickets. Non-verbal communication was of no help. Once we tried to get more toilet paper from a hotel receptionist in Hohhot in northern China. I mimicked wiping my bottom. The audience was thrilled by the spectacle, but we didn't get any toilet paper. It was easier to go to the supermarket and buy a roll ourselves.

Which of the changes are caused by traveling and which by the course of time? What would have been different if we had remained at home? It is difficult to answer as everything changes us. Probably some changes would have happened anyway, only they would have been different.

However, not everybody feels the same. French nomad Michel claims that traveling hasn't changed anything. He was laid-back before and now he is even more so. "I'm a leader. Almost nothing changed." Hobo Andy believes that the core of his personality has remained the same: he is a good man because his parents made him a good man. They took him to church, they taught him right and wrong, and they taught him that a good person is trustworthy and a bad person lies. All these value systems are intact. What has changed is Andy's global point of view.

Hobo Andy explains that his friends don't want him to be too different. The better his life has become, the more he has lost friends. Leaving can be interpreted as a rejection or a deliberate disinterest on the part of the traveler. A wandering lifestyle also forces other people to reassess their choices in life, which might make them feel uncomfortable. Is loneliness the price to be paid for nomadism?

The first time we visited Finland, I discovered a strange anomaly in the time and space continuum. According to my friends and relatives, the distance for them to travel from Finland to meet me was far greater than the distance for me to travel to Finland. Thus, I should be the one coming to see them. Defying this new law of physics has turned some of my relationships sour, but those friends and family members who care about me, visit us abroad, and when they come, they have time for us unlike in Finland where everyone has to be busy. In our visits, it has been nearly impossible to meet even our closest friends without a calendar, a mobile phone, and prearranged appointments scheduled down to the minute.

An Austrian nomad told us about the cold reception he received in his former home town some years ago. Old school friends didn't know how to deal with him. They didn't want to hear his stories but shut them out like he hadn't been away at all. Was leaving considered some kind of treason, he speculated.

As examples show, not all the lessons and consequences of traveling are positive as Rousseau already predicted. Traveling also takes something from travelers. They can never return to where they were, and they will never be able to be with the people with the same ease they used to be. Päivi believes this is what happened to one of the forefathers of global nomadism, Venetian merchant Marco Polo (circa 1254–1324).

When Marco Polo returned home and told his compatriots of his experiences abroad, they didn't believe him and thought he was a liar. Only other discoverers, Christopher Columbus and Ferdinand Magellan, believed his stories. It wasn't until six hundred years later when French scientists ascertained that Polo's observations had been truthful that he was suddenly revered as one of the first Europeans who had managed to travel to China by land.

For contemporaries, Polo was a mere storyteller and entertainer. He exaggerated, people said, and some even doubted if he had ever left home suggesting that he was just telling other people's stories. Later generations wondered why Polo failed to mention the Chinese letters, tea and foot binding in his travel account, and as the Chinese sources never mentioned Polo, this was held as a proof against him.

At home, Polo's passion for traveling faded away and he amassed himself a fortune instead. Despite the status that wealth brought him, he probably remained an outsider in the Venetian society for the rest of his life. Having had a peek at the outside world, travelers cannot adapt back to the conventional way of life pretending nothing happened, as if their world view remained intact.

Traveling can also bring along unexpected changes in global nomads themselves. We have noticed that traveling has made us intolerant. Even though we understand and accept cultural differences, we find it hard to tolerate the worst of human traits such as stupidity, materialism, greediness—and intolerance. Charity entrepreneur Anthony has noticed the same thing in himself, and it has been difficult to accept as he is at the same time promoting tolerance.

Humbleness, tolerance and willingness to engage with other cultures are one the most cherished and sought-after characteristics among global nomads. Traveling, especially in Third World countries, keeps things real and gives perspective. Sometimes the observations lead to critical self-examinations. How could one survive in an African village that has very little water and no electricity at all?

Those global nomads who return to society like hitchhiker Ludovic not only have to readapt back to the pressures of Western culture, but also translate the cultural capital they have accumulated during their travels to the sedentary. The task is not easy. How to transform immaterial lessons into money and concrete skills on the job? How to measure such things as an ability to navigate in the global world, adapt, communicate, and find one's way through hardships and obstacles? How to assure the potential employer that one's travel experiences will bring them added value?

Ludovic encountered various prejudices. Some employers had a hard time understanding what the five-year gap in his CV was about. A five-year holiday? These were not the kind of employers Ludovic wanted to have. He had originally planned to make a career in international business where his father and two brothers were also working, but during his tour he was shocked by the reality of the world. There is a saying in French that emotion is a door to conscience. Ludovic chose a job with an NGO that promotes peace through sports under the protection of Prince Albert in Monaco. He is now responsible for field projects in post-conflict areas such as Congo, Burundi, Columbia, Palestine, and Ivory Coast. "All the dangerous places," Ludovic says laughing and adds, "Although I'm back in France, my life is anything but boring."

Exploring the Earth

Thirty-nine-year-old American Max is a member of hospitality exchange. Our nomad friends had stayed with him in Florianopolis, Brazil, and they were impressed by his lifestyle. Max works in IT and has the ability to work from anywhere in the world. Every six months to a year he picks a new city, rents an apartment and lives there. This way he gets a new bakery, a new place to do his laundry, and a new set of people to hang out with. Not being a prisoner of geography, he is a prototype of an entrepreneur that the information society admires.

Nothing in Max's early years indicated that he would become a world traveler. He grew up in the countryside of Idaho where his family had a dairy farm. One of the amazing things Max recalls having done in his life was deliver a baby calf.

Max's traveling career started when he was sixteen. He hitchhiked around the United States and met a friend in Hawaii who got him hooked on the idea of going abroad. One year later Max was hitchhiking from town to town in Europe. He earned his living as a dishwasher, bartender, and waiter.

When Max returned to the United States, he studied philosophy and got hired by a dotcom company. Nine years later while living in Manhattan he wrote patents for speech recognition technology, played a computer game called Ever-Quest, and had some love affairs. Then 9/11 happened and changed everything. Max realized he didn't want to live in the United States any longer. What bothered him was the kind of police state that the country turned into. Suddenly his bags were searched in the subway and every time he got into an elevator, there was a message to be afraid.

Max doesn't nurture a great love for people who tell him how to live, where to live, and what to live. I can easily relate to his point of view after living in a Nordic welfare state where citizens are patronized to death. We also share one favorite country: France. "In the United States people are afraid of the government but in France the government is afraid of the people," Max sums up.

Leaving wasn't difficult for Max. He had had success in things Americans value, but he found his victory hollow. He started to look for something more interesting and came up with traveling and the challenge of languages. This time, however, he no longer wanted to travel on a budget. "It was a lousy way to travel even though people say that there is nothing like the shared suffering with the fellow traveler," Max jokes.

Since his departure, Max has been alternating between Europe and South America. Poland, France and Brazil are his long-time favorite countries where he enjoys returning to. When switching places, there is almost zero interruption in his work. The biggest challenge for him is organizing a high-speed internet in his apartment.

When Max was still single, he had three motivations for choosing his destinations: food, girls, and a liberal government. In 2010 when we located Max, he was dating, and his motivations and travel style had changed accordingly. He was adjusting to the idea of forethought instead of dealing with the consequences. For Max, thought and action are not separate. If he gets excited about something, he picks up his phone, buys tickets and goes; if he doesn't like the place, he leaves. Paris was on the couple's list of possible next destinations. Max likes big cities with a lot of activities going on to keep him from getting bored.

After seeing the world as a big playground, Max doesn't consider returning to the United States as a viable option. There are things in his country that Max dearly loves, but he finds the idea of America—the focus on individual rights and the feeling that anything is possible—more often in other countries than in his own. Max doubts that he can really live anywhere anymore. He has lost his innocence and cannot drop into a culture and stay there thinking that the government is good and society is kind. States and societies are just constructs for him, and he doesn't take laws, governments and cultures too seriously. Everything that is, is simply what happens to be now. It was different before, and it will be different later.

Max understands why there are visas and living permits, but he would like to be exempted from everybody else's rules. He considers himself as a net benefit for the countries he visits. He doesn't take anything from them but spends money, and he is a good citizen and doesn't create any kind of problems. Max fails to see any objective reason why anybody would complain about his presence in any particular area.

We make Max laugh when we ask what does it take to be a global nomad. He believes traveling is part of his DNA, but he vigorously denies that it would somehow be a better DNA. "It could be as much insanity as illness," he says. "A normal person would get to a place, be comfortable, build relationships and stay put." During his years of travel, Max has realized that true changes happen inside and geography has nothing to do with them. If a person is open and willing to accept what comes to him, he can be a traveler anywhere.

Max believes global nomads have a basic lack of content

where they are and egoism to pursue their dreams. Self-satisfaction and an ability to be comfortable in their own head will help in times of loneliness, and an ability to endure unpleasant times and face things is a must. Nomads have a will to complete because sometimes they have to do things and—despite all good objective measures—stick to them. Finally, a global nomad had better like people.

Throughout time, the personalities of world travelers have excited curiosity. In the old days wanderers were invited to courts to meet kings. The audience wanted to hear their stories and see with their own eyes what the well-traveled looked like. Nowadays long and exotic trips intrigue the media. Many of the global nomads of this book have become celebrities in their countries of origin.

Do global nomads have the same personality traits? No. We found among them extroverts and introverts, courageous and careful, serene and moody, gregarious and shy, emotional and logical, outdoor and indoor people. They are as versatile as any group of sedentary people. If there is one common denominator to be found, it is mobility and willingness to change. While those who prefer the status quo and feel confused, frustrated, and even frightened in the face of new things, global nomads live for new experiences. Being temporarily lost in a new city is not a reason for panic, nor is it a derailing experience from which they would protect themselves by a GPS. Instead, it can be pleasurable because being lost opens doors to the unexpected.

Embracing change also applies to identity. Nomads are not only this or that but both. Max describes the extremes of his roles: he is the president of a company meeting his customers in a suit and a tie, but he is also a member of a hospitality exchange sleeping on somebody's floor with ten other people who have been drinking all night. Yoga teacher Phoenix elaborates the theme further by saying he is a dichotomy: he negates even himself. He loves to go to Paris and buy nice clothes, but at the same time he doesn't give a damn what he wears.

Personality theories that try to fit their subjects into well-defined categories cannot grasp such contradictions. In the face of change and mobility, all labels, categories, averages, Gaussian distribution, random sampling, analysis of variance, and percentages are useless. Yet, categorizing is still among the most popular of approaches. Päivi traced the roots of this scientific method back to the eighteenth century, when Swedish naturalist Carl von Linné (1707–1778) created a system for categorizing all the plants on the planet.

Linné's discovery was revolutionary. With his method, scholars were able to label the whole world, at least in principle. Suddenly all travelers became scientists whether they had an academic background or not. Linné's example guided most travelers to practice natural sciences. They gathered plants, named new species, or identified those that had already been discovered. Also the image of a traveler changed accordingly. While he had earlier been a suffering hero who sacrificed himself in the name of science, now he disappeared into the background pretending to be a neutral and objective observer. He classified others, but was not classifiable himself—like a god on earth.

Linné became one of the icons of the time. When he traveled to Lapland in northern Scandinavia to pick plants and get acquainted with the nomadic Sami people, he walked and rode horseback carrying notebooks and a press for drying plants with him. His followers came to be recognized for the same tools which have later become travelers' fetishes in the same manner as sextants, maps, compasses, and hiking boots. Especially those who don't travel, acquire them.

On their journeys, scientists kept diaries and log books. The practice is not uncommon for global nomads either. Max has the habit of reflecting on his experiences when he changes destinations. Every four to six months after leaving a country he sits down and writes what he felt and thought, and what he discovered about the country. The distance in time is needed to view things more clearly. When Max has later read his notes, he has found insights both into his own behavior and the behavior of culture. This is one of the most satisfying parts of writing to him. When a country has truly had an effect on him, the text pours on to the page.

Constantly changing places alters the concept of home. It shifts the focus from belonging to only one country to belonging to the whole world. Max calls himself a global citizen and sees the world as his house. His kitchen is France, his recreation center South America, and his den Poland. They are just neighborhoods in his little village. The ability to feel at home anywhere awakens an interesting question: what does the word 'home' mean for global nomads?

When we asked the question to our fellow global nomads, we got various answers listed below:

- Home is defined by official documents, and it is related to nationality, domicile, passport, and tax-paying. It has no emotional connections such as warmth or a feeling of security.
- Home is four walls and a roof.
- Home is an RV, car, or boat.
- Home is products, for instance a laptop and/or files.
- Home is close relationships.
- Home is a prison.
- Home is everywhere.
- There is no home.

Most global nomads agreed there is no home. They don't have a home nor other safety nets. They are constantly on the move and at home wherever they happen to be, or—depending on the point of view—homeless.

Many global nomads define home by close relationships. For me home is wherever my loved one is. It has nothing to do with walls and a roof, or a country. For hobo Andy home is where his parents and old friends are, and for yoga teacher Phoenix home is in California where most of his friends live.

Jewelry seller Suzan relates home to feelings and reminds us of the old proverb: "Home is where your heart is." She calls herself a gypsy as she doesn't really have a home.

For Max, home is the immaterial property stored in or accessed through his computer: photos, movies, music, and connections with friends. He fights to keep geography from deciding whom he can be friends with. Max believes that by exploring the earth, "We stop being the place that we are from, the job that we do, or the experiences we have had; we become people sharing the road."

Travel Writing

When we were living in New Zealand during the second year of our journey, Päivi borrowed the book *Tales of a Female Nomad* from the public library and read it enthusiastically. Years later, in 2010, we were able to locate the author, Rita. Attempting to agree on the meeting with her was revealing of the nomadic lifestyle. Rita proposed Tuesday the 22nd, but the next day she apologized having noticed that Tuesday was in fact the 23rd. We replied to her, "No worries. Last year we celebrated New Year's Eve on December 30th."

Seventy-two-year-old Rita is an American author known for her numerous children's books that can be found on the shelves of American schools. Rita has lived on the road since 1988. The lifestyle came as a surprise not only for Rita's friends and family, but for Rita as well.

It was divorce that got Rita on the move. She asked herself what she was going to do with the rest of her life: was she going to be the kind of mother who moved in down the street and saw her children every day? Rita was too independent for that and so were her children. Rita also hated the idea of being dependent on alimony. She didn't want to give that kind of power to anyone, even if it benefited her. Thus, rather than be an embittered divorcee, like she saw a lot of women around her becoming, she decided to do something else. She redesigned her life.

Rita sold everything and took off with a backpack to discover what an extraordinary world it is. Although Rita has always loved traveling, she hadn't made many journeys during her years of marriage, because her husband was phobic about planes. When Rita no longer had to make compromises, she was free to do whatever she wanted. In the beginning she felt this new-found freedom to be a bit scary. She was scared of the smallest things like eating a meal by herself in a restaurant, because it was not something that she was used to doing. After all, Rita had thought she was going to spend the rest of her life with her husband. Rita's relatives kept thinking that she was fleeing reality with her nomadic lifestyle, but when her journey continued and continued, they eventually stopped judging her.

During her travels, Rita has overcome her fears and learned to trust. For her, trust is one of the most important elements of being happy. It is also reciprocal. When Rita walks out into the world and trusts people, she gets it back: people trust her. Rita has learned the importance of living in the present moment and seizing the opportunity. She has four tips for travelers: "Smile a lot, talk to strangers, accept all invitations, and eat everything you are offered." When an invitation comes her way, she says yes. When someone smiles at her, she smiles back. When people invite her to sit down on their porch, she often does. She accepts the cup of coffee she is offered, and she plays with children, sometimes blowing bubbles with a wand or reading them one of her stories.

Rita's career as a children's author began when she left to seek her fortune in New York after finishing college. She had majored in English literature and her first job was at a children's magazine—although not as a writer but as a file clerk. What her bosses didn't know was that Rita was lacking in organizing skills. She recalls messing up the files so badly that she was made a writer just to keep her away from the files. When Rita got married, she became a stay-at-home mom which gave her an opportunity to concentrate on writing. She also became active in the community for example protesting against the Vietnam War.

We found Rita in Washington DC where she had settled down for some time to work for her organization "Let's Get Global" which encourages young adults to make a gap year abroad after high school. Rita put her own nomadic life on hold and started the organization when she realized how isolated the United States is. "Most of the country is fearful of foreigners," Rita says and adds that if Americans are going to be part of the world, they have to know it better. "I'm convinced that anyone who goes out into this world, discovers that we are really all the same and it will be much harder to drop bombs on people who are us."

For Rita, nationalities and borders are insignificant. She is not in the least interested in being an American abroad. She is troubled by many things in the United States, among them waste and superficiality. She reminisces how she moved to Los Angeles with her husband in 1967. She didn't like the place. She didn't like the fact that she had to wear fancy clothes, and she found many of the celebrities she knew very superficial. Outwardly, Rita's life was glamorous. She ate in the best restaurants and went to the Academy Awards and the Grammys. At the same time Los Angeles made Rita realize she wasn't experiencing life.

Now Rita's main motive is to meet locals and live with them, often without any creature comforts. When she was living with a Maasai tribe in the border of Tanzania and Kenya, the huts had plugs but there was no electricity, Rita recalls laughing. Rita prefers to observe the normal day-to-day life of people instead of organized cultural events and touristy activities. She has to be dragged kicking and screaming to see this building and that cathedral as her life is about connecting. She is a tourist of human condition rather than a tourist of things.

Having visited numerous sights, most global nomads have learned to avoid them. So have we. In the end, all buildings start to look alike and feel more and more like Disneylands that are only built for making money. For anyone considering my view cynical I recommend touring from sight to sight for a year, from museum to museum and from festival to festival every single day of the year. That will probably give them an idea what I'm talking about. Global nomads would rather go to a coffee shop, meet locals who have lived there for a long time, and ask them about things which are important to them.

Rita has received thousands of e-mails from her fans after writing her nomad book. Her life is currently devoted to encouraging others, to awaken some of the spirit that lies trapped inside. It doesn't have to be traveling. For some, Rita suggests, it might be just singing out loud or sitting through three films in one day; for others, perhaps going deep sea fishing some weekend when everyone thinks they are at a church retreat.

When Rita gets her organization up and running, she will continue traveling. There are many places she hasn't been to yet, for example China, Eastern Europe, and the Pacific Islands. She is prepared to go almost anywhere and cherishes the thought that much of the world treats older people nicely—much better than the United States. Her children, however, are not so happy about the idea, but Rita is convinced they will deal with it when the time comes.

Päivi told me that traveling has long been an important part of business for artists. In ancient Greece, poets wandered from court to court selling their art and making their works known in art festivals and competitions. Tours were regulated by a market economy: artists went to those places that offered work and paid the most, and they also expected commissions along the way. As the distribution and marketing channels were undeveloped, travel was necessary for publishing, and so it is also today. Writers are expected to do road shows to sell their work.

In the old times, traveling was costly. Taxes were collected on entrance to cities and ports, and various dangers lurked on the road and on the seas: wars, pirates, and robbers. To protect themselves, poets joined associations which provided them with passports guaranteeing their safety. These associations were one of the first examples of cosmopolitanism.

Was poets' income enough? How did they survive? Even today this is one of the biggest enigmas for the people I have met during my travels. In the beginning I told people that I was not working because I didn't particularly like working. The next question was always about income, and when I said I was not worried about running out of money any time soon, people thought I was a millionaire. This changed when I realized I could pretend to be an author. That was an acceptable answer to both questions. People seem to believe that published writers make a lot of money with their books. We live on Päivi's grants while Rita lives on her royalties: "I try to live on what I earn, which is poverty level in the United States, but I can live on it very well."

Traveling was also a source of inspiration. For poets like Lord Byron (1788–1824) it was a means to attain pure existence. The journey was an inner discovery and the traveler himself the foreign land he crossed.

Byron's Romantic movement had many similarities with monk's wanderings: both traveled in order to strip life to its bare basics. Both also lacked a particular destination and searched for a vision. Monks awaited for a spiritual revelation and poets hoped it would unleash their imagination. This highlight of the journey was to come as a surprise, although it was anxiously expected. It could happen anywhere, but the Romantics preferred remote natural settings.

Traveling, for the Romantics, required discomfort, scrapes and narrow escapes. They became famous as suffering travelers like Alexander the Great. This sense of traveling is already

implied in the origin of the word 'traveling'. It is said to come
from the French word *travail* meaning work. Especially in
the old times traveling really was hard.

Today, few travel writers wander aimlessly searching for a
vision and they are not homeless like global nomads either.
In fact, travel writing is fundamentally sedentary. It is tied
to home. The stories are written for book buyers back in the
author's home country. Paying customers form the outline
and point of reference for the travel experiences.

British travel writer Bruce Chatwin (1940–1989) searched
for a balance between the expectations of his middle-class
audience and his own nomadic lifestyle. It was not easy; in
fact, Chatwin's life was torn apart by contradictory urges.
He wanted to get rid of possessions, but he adored works
of art. He considered family life as restricting and causing
anxiety, but while traveling, he longed to return home. He
presented himself as a seasoned nomad posing in photos
hiking boots hanging around the neck from a shoestring,
but he enjoyed luxury.

Chatwin is not alone. Also the authors of this book con-
tradict themselves, to the extent that they have a hard time
admitting it. For fairness' sake, we wrote the following passages about each other.

> *Päivi wants to live and travel with minimal costs but*
> *she refuses to go by foot. She ignores compassion but*
> *condemns others for the lack of it. She pretends to hate*
> *junk, but she is not ready to give up even her electric*
> *toothbrush. Traveling is an obsession for her which*
> *she has later harnessed for achieving. Also writing this*
> *book is achieving that she so despises.*
> —Santeri

> *Santeri loves the idea of a self-sufficient farm but*
> *when he has an opportunity to grow his own food, he*
> *prefers to play computer games instead. He wants to*

*see himself as insignificant but gets irritated if he is
asked to do something that interrupts his playing. He
is convinced that he doesn't get easily bored and could
stare at the wall the whole day if necessary, but if he
has nothing to keep him busy, he freaks out.*
—Päivi

Despite being writers and traveling, we have not written a
travelogue before this book. Our travel blog doesn't fall into
the conventional category either which has irritated many
of our readers. We've received hate mail, hostile comments,
and a few death threats from people who have vigorously
defended their home country or their favorite travel destination. According to the feedback from our travel blog, we
should only write about our positive experiences.

There is another tradition of travel writing which was born
from social criticism: slumming (living poorly unnecessar-
ily but paying for oneself). British author George Orwell
(1903–1950) is one of the most famous slummers. Orwell was
interested in socialist ideologies and wanted to feel what life
of the dispossessed was like. He started touring around slums
wearing rags and sleeping in homeless shelters.

Orwell initially experienced what poverty was like in
Paris where he worked in restaurants and taught English
classes. His daily budget was six francs which covered food
and accommodation. Orwell fasted but he was convinced
that the pleasure of fasting applied only to those who were
fasting voluntarily. It was altogether different for the person
who was underfed right from the start. Orwell had quite a
sense of humor. Once when he was suffering from the pangs
of hunger, he prayed to a picture of a prostitute mistaking
her for a saint.

In London, life was even more expensive. It cost money
just to have a place to sit, Orwell sarcastically observed. In
the worst case sitting down on the pavement could lead to
incarceration. Orwell slept in a homeless shelter which rather

resembled a jailhouse. Conditions inside were miserable. Fifty dirty and naked men queued to use the bathroom which had only two bathtubs and two slimy towels that had to be shared by everyone. Sleeping was also difficult. The rooms stank, beds were uncomfortable, some of the dwellers were deranged, while some tried to hit on others in their sleep.

After his initial depression, Orwell realized that poverty could also have a redeeming effect. It forced the poor to live in the present. There was less to worry about, and after experiencing the fall from wealth there was a feeling of relief born from hitting rock bottom and still being alive.

Like other tramps, Orwell spent his days downtown. He took to watching acrobats, singers, photographers, artists, thieves and con men at work. Some of the street mob were genuine professionals, while others pretended to do legal business because begging could lead to a seven-day jail sentence. For Orwell, begging was a profession like any other except that it was more honest than selling. Beggars were bumming openly and they paid for the begged money with their suffering. They caused no harm to anyone and so they deserved no one's scorn either, Orwell concluded.

People resented vagrants because they didn't earn a decent living. According to a general belief—still held today—work has to be profitable. Money and status are the great tests of virtue in society and beggars fail to pass it. Besides, as their life is just idling, it is wrong.

The cure Orwell proposed to the tramp problem was conservative: tramps needed honest, physical labor. Every workhouse should run a small farm where inmates could work and get decent food. Orwell's proposition reflected the middle-class work ethic which regarded work as a cure to all problems and a way to reintegrate the excluded or destitute back into society. Ironically, this proposition led to the kind of patronizing surveillance state Orwell later fiercely criticized in his book *Nineteen Eighty-Four* (1949). Orwell wanted to improve the lives of others based on his own experiences.

However, he wasn't forced to spend the rest of his life sleeping in homeless shelters and dodging the police in the streets thanks to his middle-class safety net.

Later in life, Orwell became addicted to slumming. When the civil war broke out in Spain, he rushed to the front to fight with the Republicans. He was not sure what it was he fought for, but he knew what he opposed: fascism.

For most global nomads the idea of someone telling others how to live is not acceptable. Rita's motto is: "You observe, you participate, but you don't try to change people." It is part of her instinct and part of her anthropology. She tries to land as graciously as she can in the places she visits, and she tries to learn from others instead of teaching them.

Global nomads might experience slumming through volunteering which can be a way to learn about the miseries of the world and to sympathize with the poor. For some, slumming might be related to their idea of equality of all people; for others, it could be a personal school of life that teaches humbleness while putting their life into perspective, and reminding them of the pleasures of a simple life.

Sometimes global nomads feel guilty about having more then the local poor people. They are free to choose where they want to be. It wouldn't be as easy to travel with a non-Western passport, and some people are never allowed to leave their countries. The guilt global nomads feel can also stem from the fact that they have had the courage to leave, while some of their friends and admirers only dream about a free life.

Why is guilt such a dominant feeling in our lives? It is produced by education and rooted in our respective cultural heritage. In many religions, guilt offers a means to control people: to make them fear, be humble, and obey. I discovered the power of guilt when Päivi and I were living in Italy. From the outside, Italians look carefree and easy-going, but inside they are tormented by various scruples. They feel guilty about not taking better care of their children or parents. They feel guilty about being unemployed or working too much, for having success or being drop-outs. When traveling, they feel guilty about being away from their loved ones, and at home they feel guilty about not seizing the opportunities they might have. The feeling of guilt is beneficial for the church because it makes people go to masses, confess their sins, and buy indulgences.

I was also pressured by guilt to work for the common good. Because of my plans to leave, I was labeled a psychopath. Some of my former friends in the Junior Chamber tried to rescue Päivi from me before our wedding. We had to tighten security arrangements at the church to ensure that the celebrations went smoothly.

Wishes for happy travels were presented in a manner that predicted a rapid return. There are many sayings in Finland reminding us of the story of the Prodigal Son, who leads a lavish life abroad and returns home poor and humbled, begging for absolution. My parents are still convinced that our journey is a flight from life and we will return to Finland to raise a family and build a house like any upright citizen in Finland would do.

Why was leaving such a bad thing? In heavily taxed Nordic welfare states—which in principle offer almost free health care, schooling, university and social security for all citizens—those who leave for good or those working abroad and returning back later in life are looked upon badly because they have not contributed to the common good. People are afraid that they will reap the benefits at the expense of others.

Society did not think there was a good reason for leaving the rat race. IT press suspected that my company was in trouble because I, the owner, fled abroad. Finnish officials got suspicious, too. When my passport expired after three years of travels, my application for a new one was initially declined. When I asked why, the answer was: "By default, the accused should know by himself what is the reason for declining his application… you must know the reason yourself and now we want to hear your comments on that." This happened one week after my memoirs were published. The book included criticism of the Finnish police and taxation officials.

None of these events and obstacles changed our minds. We figured out that by living, studying and working in Finland for thirty-four years, we had already contributed more than our fair share to society and now it was time to live our own lives. Like Rita, we redesigned our life to better fit our dreams and desires.

Challenges

WE GOT TO KNOW THIRTY-SIX-YEAR-OLD German Ingo in Buenos Aires, Argentina at the beginning of our trip. At the time we had no idea he was a global nomad—after all, we hadn't figured out any name for our lifestyle either. Ingo attended the same English group, where *porteños*, people of Buenos Aires, practiced English with foreigners. Foreigners also benefited by socializing with locals and other foreigners. Ingo was an active member of one of the many groups in the city. He had a circle of admirers and he loved to party. Everybody still remembers when Ingo sang, 'What A Wonderful World' imitating Louis Armstrong to perfection.

Ingo keeps Buenos Aires as his base and works in electoral observation missions around the world. The assignments usually last from weeks to months. Especially long assignments are profitable as Ingo gets a salary on a daily basis and his hotel costs are paid as well.

These assignments cannot be applied for through normal hiring procedures, but Ingo knows who to talk to. Because he doesn't have a permanent contract he has saved his money to buffer the irregularity of his income. Early on he was living hand to mouth, but nowadays he can manage to support himself for a year without any contract.

Ingo grew up in former East-Germany and started to travel "as soon as they let me", as he puts it. When the Berlin Wall fell and Ingo's studies in Dresden University of Technology were finished, he left to study management in the United States. He was fascinated by the country and wanted to live there. Later Ingo chose to work from Buenos Aires. He speaks Spanish fluently, and he feels accepted in Argentina. Locals consider his life glamorous because he has seen so much.

However, Ingo is not completely satisfied with his current situation. Traveling has cured his restlessness and he would now like to live a more sedentary life belonging to a community and perhaps raising a family. Ingo works as an independent consultant and he is not integrated in the everyday life of Argentinians. He has a dollar income and doesn't face the issues and problems locals do. It's a bubble. Probably many sedentary wage earners would seize the opportunity to switch places with Ingo—or would they? Would they endure rootlessness, solitude, and alienation?

Instead of working alone, Ingo would like to do something with other people. However, this requires time which poses problems because he is away most of the time. It's the downside of the job, he sighs. Ingo considers his nomadic lifestyle as transient and compares it to making a patchwork jacket. Every time he goes to a new place, he gets a new patch, but he doesn't believe patchwork jackets are as good as leather jackets made of one piece. Although his jacket looks interesting and it has got interesting stories in it, it doesn't feel like one solid life to him.

Ingo analyzes his lifestyle more critically than other global nomads. He wouldn't like to continue living in the same way for the next ten years. Traveling is tiring and he feels lonely at times. That is the significant difference between traditional and modern-day nomads. While pastoralists traveled with their community, our society is very individualized. We have been removed from our roots.

Ingo tries to grow roots whenever he is in a new place,

because nobody can be alone for long. We are not made for that. But because Ingo only stays in his destinations for a short time and doesn't necessarily return to the same place, he doesn't have the same support as people who live in a community which has been built, maintained, and fortified over decades.

Ingo considers himself partly German, partly Latin. He is quite different than Germans in a few ways: he doesn't have to plan everything three weeks beforehand, he is more relaxed, more patient, and less correct. He doesn't care what his neighbor does and he is also less competitive. In Germany Ingo appreciates the functional public transportation system, respect for rules, high-quality processed food, the high-level of intellectual discussion, and the predictability. It is the opposite in Argentina where nothing gets done unless you pay a bribe or hold an influential position.

When we lived in Buenos Aires, I noticed that locals didn't trust their society but tried to stand on their own. This is only smart from their point of view. During the financial crisis at the turn of the Millennium, when the Argentinean peso was unpegged from the US dollar, the Argentinean peso fell 4 to 1. Citizens' bank accounts were frozen, and the local citizen, not the state-run bank, was forced to compensate the difference. Someone who thought they had 100,000 Argentinean pesos now had 25,000 pesos. It is naive to trust a government who only looks after their own best interest and passes secret laws. However, when the same distrust applies to personal relationships, the result is devastating. Argentinians take advantage of each other in daily life: vendors cheat, customers leave without paying, and nobody respects agreements.

Distrust and suspicion were present everywhere. I was often asked why we had come to live in Buenos Aires of all cities in the world—couldn't we go back to Finland? After some months of defending our decision, I got fed up and started telling people we were bank robbers on the run. That stopped all further questions.

Our experiences are not unique and not only related to
Argentina. Everywhere in the world people feel uncomfortable whenever they are unable to label and classify others.
When nomads don't have a house, mobile phone, and credit
card, which are signs of respectability and credibility, it makes
other people confused.

French hitchhiker Ludovic felt like a robot on his tour,
telling his stories over and over again. It was fun for a while
but after telling the same story a hundred times, Ludovic
got tired. In Latin America, people were giving him rides
without much trouble. The fact that he is white made them
think he was rich, whereas in the United States he was looked
down on as a beggar or a bum. Another French hitchhiker,
also hitching in the USA, felt he was treated like a killer or a
rapist. Despite his sympathetic manner and appearance, he
was stopped thirty-five times by the local police and ordered
to vacate the area.

Fifty-year-old Swiss cyclist Claude has been taken either
for a criminal or a son of a millionaire on his journeys. In
Africa people asked him if the police were after him—had
he killed someone—or was his father a tycoon. When he
answered negatively to both questions, locals were vexed
and couldn't understand what he was looking for: "What do
you want? We have no food, there's nothing here," they said.

Locals are sometimes suspicious of foreigners in their
neighborhood. IT entrepreneur Max told us about the time
when the locals thought he must be a spy. Being an American
abroad still bears reminiscences of the Cold War, especially in
former East-European countries and Russia. Another American nomad recalled that where he lived in Kazakhstan and
Uzbekistan, all foreigners were spies. Locals couldn't believe
anyone came there for fun.

In a society, a clearly defined identity and stable living conditions are interpreted as necessary proofs of good character,
reliability, and confidence. A person who has no home, job,
address, phone, identity papers, bank account, and credit card

is in trouble. When French nomad Michel reported being homeless at the border between the United States and Canada, he ended up in a lengthy interrogation. "Probably it wasn't a very good answer," he joked afterward. The interrogation took forty-five minutes and the angry co-passengers of the Greyhound bus waited for him impatiently.

In Finland everybody thinks I'm not really a homeless person but a fugitive. Authorities have asked me to give my current address abroad to the Finnish magistrate, but I'm not sure if they know what they are asking for. If I sent them my address every time it changes, it couldn't be updated into the system before the next change.

In the United States, not possessing a plastic credit card can be equally troublesome as hotels might ask for hundred dollar deposits. We were not able to rent a car in Argentina for the same reason. Päivi's new credit card was sitting in Finland while the old one had expired. The credit card was required as collateral and cash was not accepted. Recently we have stumbled upon a brand new problem: most online purchases require a mobile phone in addition to a credit card. The buyer receives a security confirmation code to his mobile phone which then has to be typed into the web page. We have been unable to finalize some purchases because we don't have a mobile phone, but on the other hand, the problem is not really ours: we saved money at the expense of this particular airline company.

Lack of stable coordinates is especially hard for those global nomads who work on the way. Sometimes they have to create an appearance of stability in order to make others comfortable. Most global nomads know how to play the game: they pitch their answers to the audience.

Thirty-three-year-old American Scott described to us what it was like to search for a job as a homeless person. When he got fired from his job of running a hostel for five years, he made a three-minute decision to move to New Zealand and become a Montessori teacher. He spent three months hitching around the country, knocking from door to door at Montessori schools, and asking for a job. He was barefoot and slept in the woods every night. He smelt of the tarmac, had a knife on his hip, but no qualifications and no palpable experience. He didn't get a job.

When winter rolled around and his visa expired, Scott had two options: he could pay two hundred dollars to extend his visa, or use the ticket he already had to Australia. He had never been to Australia so he continued his voyage. Instantly, he got a hit. Still no qualification, no experience, nothing but the will to do so, but he was given a job, a place to stay and food to eat. In the interim, Scott was able to travel in his free time.

Sometimes local officials obstruct global nomads. This was already the case for pastoral nomads: governors and governments wanted to restrict their movement. Our Spanish nomad, who wanted to remain anonymous, stumbled upon the election laws of his country. If a Spanish citizen is summoned to count the votes, he must go or he will face a punishment. His bank account could be frozen and in the worst case scenario he could get a jail sentence after which finding a job in the public sector, which has most of the jobs in Spain, becomes impossible. There was no other choice for the Spaniard but to interrupt his ten-year bicycling tour and briefly visit Spain for his civic duty.

Global nomads usually don't care much what other people think of them—otherwise they wouldn't have left at all. Hobo Andy describes the attitude: "If they call me an asshole, I ask, 'What specific part in me?'" Yet, vagrancy is not always the kind of story global nomads want to discuss when speaking about their lifestyle. This storyline might be projected onto other travelers instead.

Hobo Andy warned us against heavy-duty travelers who have been on the road for more than two years. They are selfish, and they will do anything to be able to continue their travels. They are more than capable of running into debt and stealing their fellow traveler's guidebook. "These guys, they have no remorse, they are sociopaths," Andy says.

Who are these dishonest travelers? "Most of the time they become jewelry sellers and they can travel for years," Andy clarifies. When they burn all their bridges in one city, they move to the next one. They are like tramps or bums that way. Andy admits that there is a fine line between a hobo and a tramp. He feels lucky that he came from a good family and he is willing to work.

Not all global nomads want to be labeled as expatriates either. Expatriate communities are viewed to include shady and irresponsible people who have got issues that make all foreigners look bad. Locals might fear that expatriates exploit them and steal their women.

Along with people's prejudices, the topic of danger and death is always present when talking about traveling. For some, it is a motivation to hit the road, for others to stay put. I wanted to live my life so that I would have nothing to regret. What kind of memories would perpetual achieving and showing off have given me? Birth, school, studying, working, building a house, retiring—which one of these will be the best time of our life?

I believe that death shadows our lives and it motivates our actions. We do a lot of things to avoid death. We eat, we feel fear, and we try to stay safe. The will to be remembered after death and to leave something behind can influence our choices regarding family and career. What if we never died? What if we were remembered after our death regardless of our achievements? What happens to us when we die? Does death cease to exist if we stop believing in it? I haven't met any dead people to confirm to me that death really exists and is real. For me, death does not exist and we only die if we believe in death. Anyway, if I for some reason died, the whole point wouldn't matter at that stage anymore.

What is dangerous is relative. In Western countries, most accidents are domestic. Mishaps like electric shock, slipping, and tripping can be lethal even in the safety of one's home. I grew up in a country that was supposed to be a refuge shielding its citizens from disease, assault, robbery, kidnapping, rape, shooting, pirates, revolts, tsunamis, and earthquakes. The statistics, however, tell me a different story. Finland is one of the most violent countries in the European Union. We have school shootings, domestic violence, racial aggressions, and random violence caused by alcohol abuse.

Finland is naturally not the only black sheep among countries and there is nothing new in the fear of violence either. Urban life has always been regarded as potentially dangerous. Nowadays food and drinks are also health hazards. Every day we read in the news about new lethal products and ingredients that we have been consuming for decades. They cause cancer just like sun bathing, increased radiation levels, and pollution.

Also so-called safe holiday destinations can turn into war zones in a blink of an eye. When we were living in Thailand in 2006, a military coup shook the otherwise peaceful country and brought it to international headlines. We were completely unaware of what was happening until we saw the tanks and sharpshooters that had occupied the Bangkok city center on the TV news. Safe havens like New Zealand have suffered from devastating earthquakes and package tours to popular destinations such as Egypt and Tunis have been canceled in the middle of a high season because of bloody demonstrations and revolts. In Greece, financial difficulties have prompted demonstrations and bombings that might spread to other European countries. What is safe, what is dangerous?

The travel recommendations that governments issue aim at creating hysteria and keeping people at home rather than traveling abroad. There is always at least a threat of terrorism in every single country, including the neighboring ones. It is part of the panic wave that started post 9/11 and which has created significant mental and physical barriers to traveling.

When we asked global nomads where they wouldn't like

to travel, Afghanistan was mentioned a few times. It has a reputation of being dangerous, but nobody rejected the idea of visiting the country after the situation has calmed down. In fact, distinguishing between safe and dangerous countries is just contemporary colonial politics with which some countries are being oppressed.

Most global nomads are ready to visit any country in the world as they all have something to offer. Charity entrepreneur Anthony has already ticked off all 192 countries. He wanted to offer children in every country an equal opportunity to participate in his program. German Ingo has also worked for non-profit organizations. He fought against the spread of AIDS in South Africa, but he is not ready to go just anywhere. He avoids war zones and extreme poverty. Yoga teacher Phoenix avoids countries which are infested with crime and disease. He doesn't have a lot of stuff but the things he has are precious to him. He has steered clear of Africa, and he doesn't really like India either, but he has been there three times for his studies.

Some global nomads avoid countries that might not welcome them because of their race or nationality, like Venezuela or Iran for Americans. A few also mentioned closed countries like North Korea, which do not allow independent traveling. Other countries mentioned included the United States, Russia, Israel, and the Scandinavian countries. These were avoided for various reasons: political, cultural, financial, and climatic conditions.

We are happy to go to any new country we haven't visited yet as long as the visa procedures are not overly complicated and expensive. We regard visas and other entrance fees to be the best way to unwelcome travelers. However, there are a few countries we would return to reluctantly: Argentina, Kenya, and Spain, all of them because of past negative experiences. But we have good friends in these countries, so we will never say never.

As present as dangers are in the media and travelogues,

only a few global nomads mentioned them, let alone exaggerated them in our discussions. They chose not to create an aura of death-defying adventurer around themselves. Most of the risks they take are mental rather than physical. Leaving the rat race behind and living on the road is, at least from the point of view of the homeowners, one of the most risky steps to take.

How do global nomads prepare themselves for the precariousness of life? Almost half have no form of insurance. They do not believe in insurance and the illusion of security it provides. One of our American nomads joked to us that instead of social security and health care, he enjoys mental security and good health—does that count? Other American nomads also found health care merely a joke. Many mentioned that they pray Obama will fix the system. For jewelry seller Suzan health care was one of the reasons why she left. When she lost her job, she also lost her health insurance which is true for many Americans. In the end, all she got was unemployment benefits for six months and she was uninsured for years.

Insurances are businesses and, as such, rip-offs. They charge too much money for what they do and pay out reluctantly. In Finland, I had many obligatory insurances, but the companies didn't bother to handle my cases, or if they did, there was always some small print nullifying my particular case. I paid them hundreds of thousands of dollars without getting anything in return. This is not only the case for insurance companies as all businesses are fundamentally cheating: companies sell at a higher price than they buy. But in case of insurance, they create the value out of nothing.

Insurances are a way to disempower people. They create a victim cycle where people become reliant on insurance and retirement. A bought security sits on thin ice: a job can be lost, a house can burn down, and the dearly-paid insurance and life savings can vanish when companies and banks go bankrupt. The security in this world comes from understanding that there is no security.

For global nomads, travel insurance is much more expensive than for holidaymakers. This is because most insurances are tied to the social programs of the global nomad's country of origin. Upon leaving their country for an extended length of time, global nomads lose access to public services and to travel insurance in most countries. In Finland, the limit is one year, but the benefits are usually stripped even earlier. Päivi was asked to return her health insurance card months before the due date. I had already voluntarily mailed back my card years earlier after getting fed up with the bureaucracy. One thing they haven't freed me from, however, is taxes. They want me to keep on filing tax reports—for nothing.

For those global nomads who want to buy peace of mind, private companies offer insurance independent from the social programs of the home country. It can cost over 1,000 dollars a year. With the same amount of money, a doctor can be visited dozens of times on the road. Health care in some of Third World countries is cheap and of good quality. Hobo Andy had a treatment in the Philippines that cost him 150 dollars. The same would have amounted to 2,200 dollars in the United States. As long as it is not a major thing, Andy can afford to be his own health insurance.

Health insurance is not valid in countries where traveling is not recommended. For Americans, about a half of the world's countries are not covered. Hobo Andy reminds us that being a traveler is hard for someone who is afraid of dying. The risk has to be accepted. Anyway, if something really bad happens, even the best and most expensive doctors are powerless. I wouldn't want to spend my last moments on earth in a futile torment in tubes and under heavy medication. Anybody who wishes to be a traveler must be resolved to face death, wherever and however it comes as the wandering monks of old already knew.

Sometimes global nomads might buy insurance to calm down their loved ones, or insurance might be a prerequisite for getting a visa. We had to buy insurance to get a Russian

visa, but when we filed a case, the company didn't even bother
to answer us. I was naive to believe that the insurance we paid
for was anything else but Russian corruption.

Rootlessness

We had already talked to more than twenty American and European nomads and we started to see similar patterns in their lifestyle. We wondered if non-Western nomads had different values, motivations, and aims for their travels. Our wish was to find some Russian nomads as—although Russia is geographically close to Europe—Russian culture and mentality is very different. However, all our attempts to make contact with Russian nomads failed because of the language barrier. Then an old friend of ours helped us out by sending us a web address of a Russian nomad couple whose blog he was following.

Twenty-four-year-old Ajay and thirty-two-year-old Maria were in Bali, Indonesia when we contacted them. The couple began their travels separately. Ajay chose India as his first destination where he visited the Himalayas and ended up in Goa, while Maria traveled by land through Siberia, Mongolia, China, and Nepal to the same destination. They met in Goa and decided to explore the world together. They are happy they have found each other and recommend traveling as a great way to find a partner.

Before leaving Russia, Ajay studied programming in Moscow. After three years, he was disappointed in university politics and the Russian education system in general, and he left university. He was interested in music and started to work as a DJ at a club once a week. As he was still fascinated by programming, he finished his studies on his own, reading books and using the internet.

Maria is from Yakutsk, Siberia. She studied taxation and business, but she never worked in the field. Instead, she became interested in designing web pages. Ajay says Maria was one of the best web designers in East Russia, and makes Maria smile timidly with his complement. Maria is shy when it comes to speaking English, but brightens up whenever she can speak Russian.

Neither Maria nor Ajay look like Caucasians. Maria is from the Asian side of Russia, and Ajay's father is from India. Ajay always stood out in Russia which made him a target of Russian racists. During his last years in Russia, he only went out when it was pouring rain, or when the weather was so cold that people stayed inside. Being beaten up time after time and finding himself at a hospital convinced him he should not spend the rest of his life in Russia.

Ajay says he is a man without a country. Remaining in Russia was not an option for him. Besides racism and street violence, there were other problems: prices were high, the quality of life low, people were angry, and the government corrupt. "It is impossible to live in Russia without breaking any laws, because laws were created for extracting bribes from people," Ajay explains.

While Ajay was pushed into traveling, Maria left inspired by travel stories. She read travel blogs of people who had made long journeys and envied their lifestyle. Her first trip was to India for a month. She wanted to see if she would enjoy long-term travel, and she discovered that traveling wasn't hard at all. Within six months of her return, she left Russia with 5,000 dollars in her pocket. She planned to continue until her money was finished, but when she met Ajay, the couple found a way to earn their living on the road and so her journey continues.

Ajay and Maria maintain a Russian travel blog where they write stories, post photos, and sell advertisements. They are proud to say that it is the most popular stand-alone travel blog in Russia, and it has changed the lives of many people. To date, less than one per cent of Russians travel on their own, the couple says. Most buy a two-week package tour because they are too afraid of going abroad alone. With their example, Ajay and Maria want to show that anybody can travel.

Ajay and Maria spend 900 dollars a month. In 2010, their income from their travel blog was 500 dollars a month and increasing daily. Ajay also owns a small apartment in a suburb of Moscow which he is renting out. That provides the income to cover the rest of their budget. The couple has no savings nor do they want any, because more money would only mean more work, more responsibility, and more problems. With their current lifestyle, they have time for their hobbies. Maria likes handicraft, Ajay composes music, repairs his motorbike, and designs web sites.

Ajay and Maria's status has sunk in the eyes of other Russians. Although their parents are proud of them, not all of their relatives share their views. A few family members have pressured Maria to get married, buy an apartment in Yakutsk, and get a job in a bank or in a tax office. Ajay's brother and sisters think he is just wasting his time while they work, buy cars, clothes, and new mobile phones. Because Ajay doesn't have what they have, they think his life is somehow poorer. Ajay doesn't want to try to change their minds. He believes everyone should live their lives the way they want to.

Both Ajay and Maria hope to visit as many countries as they can before settling down and starting a family, but even with a family they don't want to be stationary. Children don't have to limit traveling. The couple have pondered where to settle down. Thailand or the Philippines are some of their options, but they want to see South America first. Maria likes all the countries they have visited, but Ajay boycotts one: Russia.

For Ajay, a home country is a place where people look similar and where they speak the same language. He does not belong to this kind of country anywhere. In Russia, he doesn't look like a Russian and in India, where he blends in, he doesn't speak the language.

Feeling like an outsider is not only tied to one's appearance. Although Päivi looks like a typical Finn, she never felt that she belonged in Finnish society. She tried to conform and succeeded in some of the things that are highly valued by Finns such as earning the highest academic merits. I too tried to fit into Finnish society when I founded a successful software company. However, neither of us were satisfied with our achievements. We wanted to do something that originated from our own desires, not from society or other people.

The sense of not belonging and being an outsider eased our transition to the nomadic lifestyle. When we talked with our fellow global nomads, we recognized many common experiences and thoughts although we all come from very different backgrounds, cultures, and age groups. For many—excluding those who consider nomadism as a temporary phase in life—traveling is a resignation from their society and its values, an opportunity to redesign their life.

Global nomads have chosen rootlessness in the same way as they have chosen to be homeless and jobless. Rootlessness makes things easier as charity entrepreneur Anthony said. Not belonging to any one place is being afloat, free to explore, free to choose, free to fit in and free to leave.

Since leaving Russia, Ajay and Maria have changed their perception of life immensely. They have seen different ways of living, different religions, and different kinds of people. Before traveling they thought that some things were good for them and other things were bad for them, a narrow black or white view of the world. When they encountered different cultures and different norms, their views changed. Now they accept things they would have rejected earlier. They try to live the same way as the locals and find the best sides of that lifestyle. This makes them more adaptable.

Like Ajay and Maria, I also resent xenophobic and provincial mentality in my culture. I have been flabbergasted by the news I have read about Finland since we left. Finland has never been outward-looking, but the current politicians are aiming at almost a total exclusion of foreigners. Only those who earn more than an average Finn are welcome. This excludes most of those considering immigrating to the country, because a non-white person, however highly educated, will have a hard time getting a decent job in Finland. Employers are reluctant to hire even other Westerners just like I was when I was recruiting people to my company. Finnish customers want to deal with Finns only and in their own language.

Finland has a long tradition of intolerance. When I was a child, it was normal to be racist, especially against Russians and gypsies, as long as you were racist behind their back. They had to be ignored and made to feel unwelcome in Finland. My grandparents, who had been in the war with the Russians together with their Nazi German allies during the Second World War, told me over and over again: "Russians are Russians even if you stir-fry them in butter" meaning you will never change a Russian. In the war, Finns became megalomaniacs and wanted to annex Russia to Finland. Many Finns are still afraid that Russia will seek its revenge. They desperately want to conceal the existence of the Finnish concentration camps that were in Karelia, or that we shipped Jews to Estonia for Germans to pick them up. I believe these old wounds keep feeding fear and racism and they will not heal until Finland admits and apologizes for these atrocities.

The more homogenous, monocultural, and monotheistic a country is, the harder it is to understand someone else's way of life. People who look and act different are considered a threat instead of us being considered part of the human race. We have the same basic needs as one of our American nomads says: to have a roof over our head, food in the belly, and for parents, their children to be safe. Anyone who can connect to people on this level, can be a successful traveler.

After leaving, most global nomads assess their home countries critically, but not all of them are anti-nationalist like me. For some, home country inspires nostalgia even though they are not necessarily willing to return. One of our American nomads misses American cities, scenery and nature, and starts pondering whether he should feel bad about missing places more than people. He misses Lake Tahoe, where he is from; Yosemite, where he lived for two years. He misses Ashland, Oregon, and the Shakespeare Festival. He misses the way the pine forests smell. He misses all the hot springs he knows about and the incredible skiing. He misses all the good food and he misses the wide variety of organic stores. He misses being close to Mexico, and he misses the San Francisco Opera.

All global nomads miss their family and friends, and—perhaps not surprisingly—almost as important are the kind of foods nomads grew up eating. French hitchhiker Ludovic misses the French kitchen, Canadian hitchhiker Anick maple syrup, an Argentinian nomad *dulce de leche* (caramel spread) and barbecued meat. An Israeli nomad recalls smelling the sweet scent of fresh baked pita bread coming from the bakeries in the morning.

French nomad Michel travels with a proper wineglass with a stem—a plastic one for practical reasons. Although many people drink from other kind of glasses, Michel thinks it's heretic. He kisses girls on the hand just to show them he is from France, and he is always late for appointments. Michel proudly shows his French heritage wherever he is, unless he is expressly forbidden to do so. In Norway, Michel's host prohibited him from dipping bread in tea. He feared it would give a bad example to his children.

We missed rye bread in the beginning of our trip but we have grown to enjoy a variety of other breads. In Europe we cook pasta and potatoes, in Africa couscous and *ugali* (thick maize porridge), and in Asia rice and noodles. From the Western countries we miss potable and running tap water. It is troublesome and polluting to buy drinking water in five gallon plastic containers when our daily consumption exceeds three gallons. It is also hard work to carry household water from a well under the scorching sun. When the job is done, a good bath is needed, which consumes the better part of the water carried.

Curiously, familiar shops and shopping habits are almost as important as food to most global nomads. They don't want to spend too much time and energy on everyday chores like grocery shopping and cooking. On the other hand, Päivi and I enjoy wandering around in big stores and outdoor markets. We love to make new discoveries and experiment with local ingredients. Cooking is a fun thing to do with locals and it offers an opportunity to surprise them with exotic dishes. Cooking exchange has been one of the best ways for us to get to know local people and their culture. A shared meal and long talks in the kitchen open people's hearts and minds.

When we visited Ajay and Maria in the Philippines, we learned how to cook traditional Russian raviolis called *pelmeni*. At the time, the couple lived in a spacious house on the outskirts of Dumaguete. We arrived at a peaceful, secluded neighborhood surrounded by a jungle in a fully-packed rickshaw via potholed roads. Ajay and Maria had already lived in the house for almost a year, and they later wrote us that they had decided to prolong their stay even further as they felt at home there. Despite her white skin, Asian-looking Maria blended in so well with the locals that they talked to her in their own language, Tagalog.

Through the process of traveling, global nomads develop new preferences and so cravings and nostalgia are no longer tied solely to their country of origin. Sometimes these things are missed most just because they are not available. Nomad author Rita missed sushi in Africa, and we got a craving for French cheese when we were in China. We went to a local Carrefour to get some, but we were offered yoghurt instead. The Chinese failed to understand what the yellowish smelly stuff was.

Language and the ease of communication become crucial in long-term traveling. IT entrepreneur Max misses high-speed context-sensitive English spoken by natives, but he rarely hangs out with other native speakers. He doesn't seek out Americans or Brits, because he dislikes the typical expatriates who just sit in the bar complaining how everything is better at home.

Hobo Andy misses the everyday politeness of Americans. He recalls greeting a hotel receptionist in Estonia and asking how she was doing. The girl answered stiffly—as in English class at school—saying, "Fine thank you, and you?" When Andy asked what the girl was going to do that day, she said sulkily, "Nothing much, I'm working." For me, this conversation would have been business as usual. The same scene happens in Finland every day. Northern people rarely engage in conversation with strangers nor express any enthusiasm. Life is supposed to be grim and whoever states otherwise, is badly mistaken. A Finnish anecdote about two guys who went to the bar clarifies this mentality. They sat down, ordered two pints of beer and drank. After a while, they ordered another round and emptied their pints, again in complete silence. Finally one said to the other, "Should we order one more?" The other guy got irritated and replied, "Did we come here to drink or to talk?"

Coming from a small town in America, Andy had learned a different approach. He believes everybody needs a hug, everybody needs a bit of friendship, and everybody needs intimacy. He finds it sad that people go on vacation and ignore everybody.

Facing different cultures is one of the biggest challenges

of traveling. It is confusing. For us, the question, "What the f*
are we doing here?" is common in our internal dialogues. We
asked the question last time in Kenya and Tanzania. Whenever we walked outside, people called us mzungus (white),
or they tried to hawk us souvenirs. When we politely refused,
they started begging: "Give me your shoes… or that shirt…
fifty cents for soda… it's a cheap price… Well, you have to
give me at least something…"

Traveling in places where we are continuously harassed or
hated because of our race, skin color or nationality is tiring.
In Africa, we probably got at least a hint of what it feels like
to be a foreigner in Finland. Discrimination based on white
skin color is rarely spoken about, but for many global nomads
it's part of everyday life. Cyclists have had stones thrown at
them when they cycled in some African and former Soviet
Union countries. One cyclist speculated the reason why this
happens by saying that perhaps throwing stones was a local
substitute for the Playstation—locals were frustrated and
had nothing else to do. When he stopped to talk with them,
they were OK with him.

Americans have experienced discrimination because of
their nationality particularly during the Bush era. When
jewelry seller Suzan was in Egypt, she had to go to a hospital.
She had stepped on a coral and her foot had become infected.
It was a tiny little hospital with two employees and a camel
tied up out front. While the doctor was giving her the shots for
her infection, he was also scolding the United States. Suzan
felt uncomfortable with his treatment.

Other countries where American nomads have felt
discriminated against include France, British West Indies,
and Venezuela, and sometimes it is other travelers who are
prejudiced against the country. Suzan recalls an experience
in Cambodia where a fellow traveler, after hearing she was
from the United States, said, "Oh, you're American, I'm so
sorry." Not everybody can separate the individual and the
government.

Hobo Andy reminds us that the effect of nationality is always relative. The British consider Americans as peasants, the Dutch as equals, the Scandinavians as uneducated. For Andy, there is no culture that is better than another. There are cultures that are more honest but at the end of the day, it's just a different channel.

We had problems in neighboring areas of western Russia and Scandinavia because of our Finnish nationality. From the Finnish border until Saint Petersburg, Russians called us chukhnas which translates more or less to a stupid person, but the further east we went, the more exotic and interesting we became to locals. Other Scandinavians consider Finns to be violent alcoholics who take their knives out when they are drunk and start to fight. When we visited a Danish couple, we had come prepared to make dinner for our hosts. I searched the kitchen looking for a cutting knife and when I didn't find one we chopped up the vegetables with cutlery. I wondered why there were no cutting knives in the house and learned later that our host had hidden them, as well as his whiskey and wine bottles. He had been living in Russia for years and remembered how Finnish construction men always started a knife fight when they were drunk. He expected the same from us.

During our travels, I'm often asked if I'm German. It is not surprising as I look a lot like a German in my camouflage trousers and my shaved head, and Germans also travel a lot. We have also been mistaken for Americans, British, Mongolians, Russians, and Swedes. We were on the receiving end of an angry outburst when we were mistaken for Americans and called gringos by a couple of drunk co-passengers on a bus. Usually when people ask about my nationality, I prefer to say I'm a world citizen although this doesn't help much as it doesn't satisfy their curiosity. New questions inevitably follow.

As foreigners, global nomads always stand out. To what extent, varies according to the continent. The majority of them are Westerners who blend in fairly well everywhere

else but in Africa, Asia, and South America, but discrimination can be encountered at home, too. Yoga teacher Phoenix,
who has black hair and darker skin because of his Greek
genes, has noticed that his looks sometimes affect people's
attitudes towards him. Even the length of his hair makes a
difference. When Phoenix was hitchhiking in South America,
people called him a "hippie". It made him angry: "I could
see that people were scared." Hippie is in many countries a
defamatory word that lacks a clear definition. It can refer to
a dirty, disheveled long-haired person who is uneducated,
or to a foreigner in general. We were once called hippies in
France and thrown out of a shopping mall because of our
big backpacks.

Foreigners looking for companionship sometimes encounter racism. A foreign man and a local girl seen together are
immediately associated with prostitution. The mentality of
the local is that no normal person just becomes friends with
a white person. However, if the foreigner is rich enough, that
point of view will be overlooked.

Most global nomads are familiar with double pricing
where foreigners have one price and locals another, usually
significantly lower price. Some regard it as discrimination,
for others it's business as usual: Don't let the stupid keep their
money. Sometimes shops might refuse to serve foreigners,
and hotels might close their doors to them.

Any reason is valid for the basis of discrimination. Being
rich or poor alike can cause discrimination; a man who likes
children may be seen as a pedophile; women traveling alone
can get either discriminated against or harassed. Yoga teacher
Phoenix recalls being discriminated against for being poor in
hospitality exchange. The hosts were disappointed when they
realized that he and his girlfriend didn't have jobs. Phoenix
believes that when people get to know him, they are bound
to like him. He is not a hippie but educated and willing to
learn local languages and cultures.

Disparities of wealth are tied to social status which puts

some people above, others below. It is part of everybody's life regardless of the country or race. Hobo Andy explains what status is in the Dominican Republic: People are somebody if they have a motorcycle and they are nobody if they don't have it. The expatriates, on the other hand, are somebody if they buy a car and a house. For Andy, racism is just a minor problem compared to seeking status.

Most global nomads prefer not to share their negative experiences. Nomad author Rita thought she heard wrong when we asked her if she had been discriminated against. Some wanted to forget their experiences saying that the good always outweighed the bad. They probably thought other races had suffered so much more than they had that it wasn't reasonable to complain. IT entrepreneur Max burst out laughing when hearing our question: "I'm white, Anglo-Saxon, six and a half feet (two meters) tall. If I was discriminated against, I guess I just didn't notice it."

Is being a foreigner always positive? There are limits to the tolerance of even the most open-minded and masochist traveler. For the sake of peace of mind and comfort, it is best to choose countries with less frictions at least for a longer stay. Päivi wouldn't want to reside in a country where people refuse to speak to women and I would have to conduct even the smallest of everyday transactions. It would cause us too much cultural fatigue.

We experience cultural fatigue when we have to adopt to norms that are different from our own. Queuing is an insignificant-sounding issue which nonetheless produces continuous cultural fatigue for Westerners for example in former Soviet Union countries. Russians have spent most of their lives in queues and they have mastered the art to perfection. The queue in front of a ticket office is only a part of the truth. Russians come and go, and they agree with their neighbors to keep each other place. Old *babushkas*, grandmothers, are masters at cutting in line. They pretend to come to ask somebody, anybody, something but instead make their way to the queue. Polite Westerners can easily spend an eternity in a queue that keeps growing right before their eyes.

Many people don't travel abroad at all because they are not able to deal with cultural fatigue, or they try to change other cultures. Both options are equally undesirable. If we don't encounter other cultures, we never learn to understand their upsides, neither do we learn to scrutinize our own culture critically. If, on the other hand, we try to change the other culture, we just waste our time and cause unnecessary friction by making locals feel that their culture is somehow inferior.

Cultures cannot be changed, developed, or civilized; they have a right to be different. This is not the same as accepting everything that happens in them. We don't have to accept the obligation of wearing of *burkha* in Arab countries, but we don't have to despise locals, preach our beliefs, or try to convert them while wearing bikinis. They have a right to their customs whereas we don't have the right to consider ours better. Hobo Andy says, "Just because somebody has a nice house doesn't give him the right to tell a person who lives in a grass hut what to do, and just because someone has money doesn't mean that he can remove other people's rights."

Global nomads are constantly in situations that challenge their norms, but they learn to cope with cultural fatigue. The most important thing is to live and let live, and to learn as much as possible from those things that are good in other cultures. If the experience is too much, global nomads can always leave the culture and return later. Time evens out first impressions and helps global nomads also to see the upsides of the culture.

Russians Ajay and Maria have learned an unbeatable way to overcome any problems during their travels: smiling. In the beginning they just tried to stay calm and optimistic, but then they noticed that Asians, whatever the problem, always smiled and solved their troubles by smiling. They tried it and it worked. Now smiling comes naturally to them. We learned the same trick and remembered that nomad author

Rita also advises travelers to smile a lot. The road teaches everybody the same important lessons regardless of where they come from.

Return

Cycling nomads are well networked and most of those who have traveled for a long time know about each other or they have met on the road. We got to know fifty-year-old Swiss Claude through a Finnish cyclist who had followed his blog. Claude is a veteran who has bicycled in eighty-six countries for fifteen years. For him, the most difficult part of his journeys was not traversing challenging terrains and dangerous countries, but returning home.

When Claude came back from his latest journey, he had no job, apartment, or insurance. His girlfriend, who had been his travel companion, broke up with him, and the economic and media context in Switzerland had changed considerably. Claude found it more difficult to live in Switzerland on the income he made from the conferences he was giving and his writing.

Claude still writes for a Swiss newspaper, but he has new projects in mind. He was planning to write a cycling guide about Geneva-Lausanne area with a friend of his, and he is keenly following the plans for setting up a big collective bicycle project in Geneva. The idea is to build a bicycle house of various associations which would teach and offer possibilities for recycling bicycles. Claude would like to have a library collection specializing in cycling and find himself a stable job. Yet, nobody knows when these projects will start and how big they will be.

After his return, Claude has started to think about his future pension. It worries him a bit. He doesn't believe he will be able to live in Switzerland on the little money he will get. So far he has just continued on without thinking, but now he is already fifty. Claude doesn't want to trade his freedom for wage slavery. He has never earned much, but he wants to be independent. On his tax report, Claude's official status is a *cyclonaute* and a globetrotter.

Cycling for Claude has been the best way to express who he is. He is not an artist but that is the closest correlation he can think of. A painter will paint even if he breaks his arm, because painting is his life. It's the same for Claude. If he couldn't ride anymore, he would be unhappy with life.

Claude lives in Geneva. Although travelers have big wings, they also need roots, he claims. Claude has been speaking with old sailors who eventually want to die where they were born. Claude thinks it's genetic. There are very few people who emigrate happily and fall in love with a new culture. Most are linked to a very precise point on the planet.

Claude has raised his standard of living while society pressures have required individuals to own more. He regrets the amount of stuff that being sedentary seems to require: car, computer, kitchen, pots, pans, and books. Returning global nomads also have to accept the bureaucratic paperwork: rent, phone, electricity, gas, water, taxes, vehicle insurance and credit card payments. Is the whole set-up "an outrageous swindle, a blatant and egregious con-job," as British travel author Richard Grant rants?

Friends and family ties are what Claude enjoys most about being at home. His parents are old and as they lost his elder brother, he is the only remaining immediate family. He feels he has to spend more time with his parents now. If he went to the other side of the world, maybe one of them or both would die.

Claude doesn't consider himself a typical Swiss although he enjoys living in the country. Whenever he has left home, Switzerland has also been his destination. His whole life has been a big detour which has helped him to understand the world and himself. Claude loves the Alps. When traveling, he is always looking for other mountain areas, such as the Andes and the Himalayas. Claude sometimes wonders if he selects the places or if they select him.

Claude denies being nationalistic. He doesn't agree with everything that happens in his country. When he was twenty years old, he was in jail because he protested against military service. However, deep inside he feels quite satisfied in Switzerland. It is a rich and well organized society. Where else could he earn his living by writing and telling about his travels?

When cycling around Geneva, Claude often meets people who recognize him. He is not a film star or a politician, but people want to shake his hand and say that his travels are great.

For some global nomads, roaming around the world is a temporary phase in life. They go back to their countries, work, find themselves a partner, and start a family. These plans, however, are fuzzy at best, and it is likely that they will change many times. British travel writer Chatwin predicted that restlessness will always drag travelers back to the road, and if wanderlust is for some reason suppressed, it finds undesirable outlets such as violence, greed, status-seeking endeavors or a mania for the new. Chatwin himself ended up zigzagging between departures and arrivals.

Although some of the global nomads had started their travels thinking it would be a temporary phase in their lives, they had later changed their minds. Others might have tried to make a comeback, but then decided to continue traveling like our Argentinian nomad. At home he gained weight and felt bad and decided that he doesn't want to try to go back anymore. The place had changed, he had changed, and it was a different situation altogether. Those global nomads who had decided to return home but had not yet done so, had made their decision recently. Time will tell if they will return or keep on traveling.

French hitchhiker Ludovic is one of the rare ones that seem to be happily rooted after their travels. He always knew that when his tour was over, he would have to turn the page and start a new life. Ludovic found a wife from Panama who made settling down easier. The couple kept in touch through the internet while Ludovic thumbed his way around the world. When the tour ended, they tried out living together first and then got married. The couple intends to stay in Southern France and start a family. They travel, but not by hitchhiking as Ludovic's wife prefers a more conservative mode of transportation.

Those global nomads who consider return, worry about what will happen to the things they have learned during their travels. They have been happier on the road and they have adopted a lifestyle that suits them, but they are not sure if they can maintain it back home. Will the lessons learned and harmony gained vanish in the midst of consumer-mania, routines and the hustle of everyday life? Traveling teaches asceticism, downsizing, and ecological consciousness. Maybe some of these practices can be transformed into the daily life, but it could also be like swimming against the current.

Claude and some other global nomads seek a holistic lifestyle to combine work and personal interests. Claude would like to work with bicycling; a Mexican nomad hopes to open a hostel on the beach in his home country and employ locals; Canadian hitchhiker Anick wants to earn her living by lecturing and writing about hitchhiking. People who turn their hobbies into work are usually admired, but what are the consequences? Does the attraction remain? I'm skeptical. I turned my hobby, computers and software, into a career and I was soon occupied with secondary nonsense: management, sales, and bureaucracy. At the end of the day, I had very little time for the things I enjoyed. Perhaps the situation would have been different, if I had just focused on writing free software and exploited social security to make my living instead of starting my own company.

The dreams of having a career and a family are most common among young travelers. Those who have already had their experiences of sedentary life rarely look back. The novelty value has faded. However, when following the paths of other global nomads we have sometimes been surprised by the choices they have made.

A couple of months after our discussion, yoga teacher Phoenix, who had been studying at university, finished his master's degree and accepted a full-time job as an English teacher for foreign soldiers on a military base. Although the work was antithetical to what he believed in, he was tired of being broke. It was a high paid job and something he had studied for. Phoenix had also found a new love, Jennifer. When she became pregnant, Phoenix was perplexed what to do. After initial shock and a lot of soul-searching, he decided he wanted to have the baby. Now the couple is saving money to be able to move to New Zealand and buy land. The line between the sedentary and the nomadic is thin.

Half of the global nomads we met continue to travel without any plans to stop. For some, the whole idea of returning back to society is repulsive. When our friends and former colleagues in Finland have urged us to return, I have replied that I would rather stick my head into a toilet seat and lick it clean. But I couldn't resist the temptation to fulfill other people's expectations about our return. For an April fools' joke I told my friends we were moving back to Finland because I was running for parliament, and I asked them to give me tips on houses with a sea view in downtown Helsinki. I was bombarded with questions, support, and congratulations.

Most global nomads have invested so much into their lifestyle that the prospect of returning home is no longer attractive. One of our American nomads plans to slowly fade away from society. He knows he will always carry society with him, but a society he creates himself of those he loves around him. Another American nomad wonders why people speak about return at all as if it is the global nomads who are the rogues or misguided. The nomadic lifestyle opens so many doors and opportunities that it would be a waste to close them again. Why not encourage departures instead?

Departures require arrivals and arrivals departures. Stories live in-between. When we next time heard from Swiss cyclist Claude, he was feverishly planning a new trip from Kirkenäs via Helsinki to Istanbul, 4,350 miles (7,000 kilometers) along the former iron curtain. Geneva was, once again, only a stop-over. Our Argentinian nomad friend had returned to his mother's house in Argentina and yoga teacher Phoenix had applied for a job in Ecuador.

Are global nomads tourists who are just on a exceptionally long world tour? Claude believes we are all tourists whether we are on a package tour or on a nomadic exploration. He feels it is snobbish that nomads want to be different. Claude has sometimes stumbled upon groups of tourists coming out of the bus with their cameras, and some of them have been much more sincere and honest than travelers who brag to have "been-there-done-that." Claude reminds us that the world was invented by the British in the eighteenth century: "We are not inventing anything. We just buy tickets."

Those global nomads who are traveling without plans to stop can be more critical about tourism. For them tourists represent the society they have left behind. They have very little in common. Yoga teacher Phoenix views tourism as an attitude. Tourists try to take as much of their own country with them as they can. They are in a foreign country, but they try to live like they are in their own country.

Russians Ajay and Maria are seemingly horrified at the

thought of being considered as tourists: "No, never!" Ajay
illustrates the mentality of Russian tourists saying that most
of them are rich and rude. They think local people are stupid
and they treat them like slaves. If locals don't understand
Russian, they just shout louder. Ajay and Maria rather speak
of *traveliving*. They want to take their time, settle down for
a while, rent a place, and get to know the cultures they visit.

When does nomadism turn into sedentary living and
the other way around? The question is not how often global
nomads stop on their way or for how long, because settling
down temporarily in a new place is also traveling. Everything
at their new destinations is strange and different.

We have developed the habit of sharing an apartment with
locals when we stop and rest for a couple months. For us it has
proved to be the best way to explore cultures from the inside.
When living together, nobody can keep up the appearances
for long. Consequently communication becomes easier and
more genuine. We see the ups and downs of ordinary people
in ordinary settings.

No matter how global nomads travel or what they think
about tourism, they still impact the industry as admired
role-models for backpackers and other travel freaks. Global
nomads might also take advantage of tourism infrastructure
which makes living and moving around easier. Thanks to
tourism, roads are built, public transportation is developed,
hotels and holiday houses are constructed, and locals' language abilities are improved. When this infrastructure attracts
travelers to destinations, supermarkets, service providers,
restaurants, and coffee shops follow.

Tourism creates not only good infrastructure. Places that
have become wealthy from tourism attract street vendors,
fortune-seekers, and thieves. For our nomadic friends the
main problem lies in the assumption that all tourists want
to visit sights, sleep in hotels, eat in restaurants, hire taxis,
and buy souvenirs. When global nomads fail to fulfill these
expectations, they invite trouble or at least perplex locals

thoroughly. Why would anyone travel if he doesn't want to see the very best of the destination and enjoy his valuable free time throwing money around lavishly?

Foreigners are a source of income. Hobo Andy elaborated on the problem by saying he is a big dollar sign that walks. He was quite agitated by hawkers in the Dominican Republic. "It's time to recognize I'm a person," he remarked sourly. Andy heard the same aggressive sales pitch every day. He found it annoying, especially because hawkers didn't recognize his face. They didn't pay attention to people, money was all they were interested in.

Being constantly milked is a frustrating experience. When we have been in places crowded by tourists, we have found it hard to be patient and politely shrug off souvenir and massage vendors day after day. I have tried various strategies. In Brazil, I made us T-shirts saying, "Não obrigado," no thank you in Portuguese. Some of the vendors understood the message, laughed, and left us in peace, but not everyone could read. In Cambodia, the daily approaches of *tuk-tuk* drivers was relaxed enough to give us the patience to smile and explain that we love walking. After nine months, it was the drivers who got fed up and finally proposed to take us to the airport for free so that we would leave. In Kenya, the amount of daily offers was so overwhelming that we got tired. We ended up walking and jogging at sunrise when locals, who were afraid of dark, were still hiding in their homes. At other times we moved to the other side of the road if there were any kiosks or shops in sight, or changed direction if someone started to walk towards us on the beach. We rather avoided confrontation than ended up being nasty.

The easiest way to get rid of vultures is to get rid of money and property. Even pickpockets cannot steal anything from an empty pocket. The same applies to beggars. If we have less property than the beggar, we will not suffer from a bad conscience for not helping him, and if we really want to give the beggar something anyway, we can always give him our T-shirt.

The beggar is probably really in need if he accepts a sweaty shirt instead of money. Unfortunately, this doesn't always apply. In Bolivia beggars were circulating between restaurant tables asking for customers' leftovers. We saved some salad for them, but it was not good enough. They wanted meat. In Cambodia, a similar scene repeated itself, only this time the bones that still had meat on them were rudely refused. The beggar wanted money.

The contradiction between easy living and the mental burden of tourism is always present. That frustration can find an outlet in local culture, tourism, or other tourists. Because everybody wants to be conscious and ethical travelers, they cannot criticize locals. Thus the anxiety can only find an outlet in other tourists. This is where the widespread tourist angst, the deep feeling of anxiety, springs from. The angst is further deepened by the feeling that tourism is inauthentic, plain reproduction and kitsch. Yes, nothing truly pure and authentic can exist, because authentic and inauthentic are only different sides of the same coin. A work of art can only become genuine after the first forgery has been produced.

For some people global nomads are only fashion-conscious imitators of traditional nomads. On the other hand, the tourism industry has recruited various people and groups into its service, among them are the ancient nomadic tribes. The Maasai living on the border of Kenya and Tanzania have become tourist attractions along with wild animals. They let themselves to be photographed for money, they present their camps to tourists, and they perform folk dances and shows of blood-drawing from cattle. Other pastoralists have found jobs as hotel and camp site workers, night guards, hiking guides, safari tour organizers, and souvenir hawkers. As always when money intervenes, fortune-seekers follow. In Kenya, we often met members of other tribes in Maasai dress and beads. Everybody wanted to make money. Who was genuine and who was fake?

The Meaning
of Life

ONE EVENING ON THE ISLAND of Borneo, our writing was interrupted by a splash of water. The rain water collection system was leaking and I had to place some buckets under it. A cute little baby rat had slipped into the bucket of water and was now fighting for his life. I lifted him gently up to safety. Later I discovered that he had four curious siblings who sometimes came to peek at us. I started to give them a slice of our freshly baked morning bread, plus all our leftovers of the day. Sometimes at night they raced around on the ceiling and played with each other. It never disturbed us—on the contrary—this was the kind of rat race we enjoyed tremendously. We certainly miss our little friends.

What are the life philosophies of global nomads? If the meaning of life is not money, work, family and being a proud homeowner, what is it? Most global nomads emphasize happiness, which for them is related to traveling, new experiences, and the possibility to be present and seize the moment. Life is short, and as global nomads' interests are wide-ranging, they want to live it to the fullest.

Thirty-nine-year-old Mexican Alberto feels lucky. He is not sick. He can travel and work, and he has all of his body parts. He feels sad because many people cannot travel even if they have money. They are not healthy nor are they happy.

Twenty-seven-year-old Japanese cyclist Taro laments that people are too busy to live their own lives. He wanted to do something different and started to cycle. Sometimes his parents ask him to stay home, but Taro goes anyway. He doesn't want to be a company man.

Global nomads follow their individual desires rather than the values of their society. For them, leaving has been a statement and a conscious detachment from their society. Even if people advice them against traveling, it is not working and saving money that they want. They prefer to experience as much of this world as possible.

Global nomads believe everybody should be able to choose their own way and respect other people's right to make different choices. If working and money make some people happy, let them make a career and a fortune. For charity entrepreneur Anthony the most important thing is to take everything out of the experience—whatever it is—because there are no second chances.

Portuguese Ciro laughs at our question. He was afraid that we would ask him something like this. He ponders for a moment what to answer but his girlfriend saves him from the tricky situation by proposing that the meaning of his life is to make her happy. I find it a good answer, too. For us, the meaning of life is love and making each other happy. We cherish every moment we are together.

Fifty-three-year-old British Glen tries to make her time count for herself and for the people she is with. She has been traveling happily with her husband Steve. They are best friends, together 24/7, and maybe because they met when they were very young, they grew up together. Glen feels she is very lucky. At the end of 2011, when the couple had traveled fifteen years, Steve began feeling weak. A local hospital diagnosed Steve to have a acute lymphoblastic leukaemia. The couple had to halt their journey and sell their camper van. Merry traveling transformed into painful chemotherapy sessions, endless waiting, and uncertainty. In the midst of the fear of death, fear of loosing Steve and despair, Glen found happiness from the fact that they had managed to experience so much together and live their life-long dream of traveling. Had they done what many people do and put off traveling until later, they would probably never have realized their dream.

If there is wisdom to be met with on the road, we have noticed that it always comes from our fellow travelers and human beings. For nomad writer Rita, the meaning of life is about connecting and recognizing being human. "We don't have to dig very deeply to find out that we have the same emotions, the same concerns whether we come from Papua New Guinea or the United States," she says.

Yoga teacher Phoenix points out the contradiction between individuals and society. He grew up in a society where the goal was to earn as much money as you could, to get as much social status and power as you could, and by any means necessary. But he thinks the true goal, the true meaning of life, is to give as much as you can to other people.

Society is probably what home-coming global nomads most fear. During travels, they have had a chance to live according to their values of giving and sharing, but returning back threatens to take that away from them. Is it possible to live happily in the midst of busy, materially driven society, or is it better to remain outside?

Twenty-nine-year-old British Helen, who went back to the UK after her travels, didn't believe that her example could have any influence on anything or anyone. Now she has begun to see her inspiration in others. Her motto is: "Be the change you want to see in the world." She wants to be the good person who is generous to all that she can be. She wants to take every day as it comes and deal with what is in front of her right now. Yesterday is gone, tomorrow isn't here yet, all we have is today.

Russian Ajay wants to make more people smile and raise children who will do the same. For his partner Maria, the meaning of life is in life itself, in the present moment. It's about living it now, and not only dreaming.

Canadian hitchhiker Anick focuses on self-development. At some point she thought the meaning of life was to be happy, but then she realized that she quite likes to be torn and passionate. She used to be a bit of a Buddhist and tried to keep her passions down. Now she attempts to do her best and develop herself, but she doesn't mind changing this definition if someone has something better in mind.

Swiss cyclist Claude is uncertain. Perhaps the meaning of life is to be alive, to breathe, to share with other people, and to give and receive love. Jewelry seller Suzan tries to leave a positive imprint on the universe on some level, but sometimes she finds it difficult to answer the question as she is not sure if she is fulfilling her task. Twenty-six-year-old French hitchhiker Jérémy is looking for the meaning of life from his travels, and twenty-seven-year-old Finnish cyclist Jukka believes that things have to be really bad if one has to consider such fundamental questions.

Not everyone wants to give life a meaning. For French nomad Michel it is certainly not life after death. Obviously life will end badly. If he had been asked, he would have chosen not to be born at all, and so he would have chosen not to die either. Sixty-one-year-old American Tor can't think of any meaning except perhaps to amuse our creator. The creator is having a dream and if there's meaning it is to amuse himself, he elaborates. We're all just little figments of the universal imagination.

The scientist inside IT entrepreneur Max denies that life has any meaning. There are just random processes. The other side of him assumes that perhaps there is an intelligence in the universe that is moving to a greater level of complexity and entropy. Max studied philosophy and noticed that the great minds failed miserably in answering the question either saying it's god, or saying they have no idea but here's a fun way to look at it. It took a huge pressure off him. As a child, he thought he had to have an answer to the question but now he knows that even if he fails, he is in great company. Max laughs and adds that we have to live, answering the question is not the most important thing.

Traveling gives nomads time to think, and seeing different cultures opens up new points of view. Is it time to revive this ancient tradition which has been marginalized for centuries? Our Argentinian nomad ponders that the majority of human history is nomadic, and it is only in recent history that man has settled down. Staying put is a learned thing, a creation of agriculture, surplus, political structure, and specialization. Maybe the natural tendency of people is to be nomadic and we are only cultured and socialized into being sedentary.

If modern-day nomadism is considered to be luxury traveling, then luxury should be defined in terms of mental rather than financial characteristics. Global nomads travel with a modest budget. Their most important capital is the ability to question, to have the courage to make their own choices, and to overcome fears. Could these be new currencies for the humankind offering immunity against boom-bust cycles and inflation?

Overview

AFTER GETTING TO KNOW ALL thirty global nomads we discovered that their thoughts started to resemble each other suggesting we had reached a critical mass. Looking for more global nomads was no longer necessary.

It is time for the summary: lies, big lies, and statistics. Please be advised that the following statistics cover only the particular group of global nomads we found and therefore the statistics cannot be generalized. They are not based on a random sample of the group. Our current estimate of the total number of global nomads is in the hundreds and it probably remains under one thousand, but nobody knows for sure.

The global nomads we met ranged in age between twenty-four and seventy-two years in the time of the interview in 2010. Approximately one third of them were under thirty (8), one third between thirty and forty (11), and the rest over forty (11). There were seven women and twenty-three men, and four were traveling as a couple.

Global nomadism is a Western phenomenon and consequently the traditional pastoral nomadic areas in Africa, the Middle East, and Central Asia are not represented. Our nomads originate from seventeen countries: Argentina, Austria, Belgium, Canada, Finland, France, Germany, former East-Germany, Great Britain, Israel, Japan, Mexico, Portugal,

Russia, Spain, Switzerland, and the United States. The majority are North American followed by Europeans. Eventually we managed to locate some global nomads from South America, Asia, the Middle-East, and Russia to broaden the spectrum of nationalities.

Country of origin

USA	9
France	3
Canada	2
Germany	2
Great Britain	2
Russia	2
Other	10

Global nomads started to wander the world for various reasons. Some dropped out of school or went on the road right after school like yoga teacher Phoenix. Others first studied, made a career, got fed up with the rat race and left like us. For some global nomads, including jewelry seller Suzan, a life crisis such as unemployment, divorce, or a death of a close relative triggered a search for an alternative lifestyle. A few middle-aged or elderly women first had a family, raised children, and started to travel after their children left home. This was the case of nomad author Rita. Finally, some of the global nomads have been building their careers along the way like Russians Ajay and Maria.

Profession before traveling

Student	27% (8)
Entrepreneur	17% (5)
Social and healthcare	10% (3)
Other	47% (14)

Nomads' former professions range from waitress to CEO. Most have a higher education, usually a master's degree. Not all the degrees were finished, however. The majority of the degrees are from economics and engineering sciences. Other fields include biology, biophysics, geography, geology, journalism, literature, music/composing, philosophy, and taxation. Two of the global nomads joined the navy when they were young, but neither continued on to pursue a military career. Other professions include biologist, DJ, hostel manager, jack of all trades, real estate broker, salesman, management consultant, radio person, PR agent, gardener, office worker, video producer, and web designer.

Most global nomads travel alone. Only one third are traveling with a partner and five had had temporary partnerships lasting from days and weeks to some years. Ultimately, their paths forked because their goals were not compatible. The other person, for instance, wanted to build a career and have a family, while the other wanted to continue traveling.

None of the global nomads have traveled with a friend for an extended period of time. The travel styles of global nomads differ considerably from hobo style. Hobos formed close partnerships because of safety, frugality, and company whereas global nomads prefer independence. Global nomads do not form communities of like-minded souls either like lifestyle migrants for example in Ibiza (Spain), Mykonos (Greece), Goa, and Varanasi (India). Global nomads travel among their sedentary counterparts, and their communities can be found in temporary places to rest where they might share a house with locals. For shorter visits, hospitality exchange offers global nomads a venue to meet locals. Members of these groups appreciate long-lasting relationships instead of the use-once-and-throw-away type of acquaintances found at hostels.

Our global nomads have visited 9–192 countries. One third (11) has been in less than 25 countries, a half (14) in 25–75 countries, and the rest (5) in more than 75 countries.

Among the most popular travel destinations are Europe, North America, and Oceania. After that come North and South-East Asia, Africa, and South-America. The least popular are the Middle-East and Central Asia.

The majority of global nomads (67%) use public transportation such as airplanes, trains, buses, and ferries. The rest hitchhike, cycle, drive their own car or RV, or sail. Some rent a car or a motorcycle for a period of time at their destinations. Also more exotic vehicles are sometimes used such as cargo ships, canoes, donkeys, and camels.

Everybody has their own favorite mode of transportation but the choices are limited according to what the destination has to offer. Freedom and independence are some of the main criteria for choosing a particular vehicle along with cost and schedule. Also speed matters. Some want to travel as fast as possible in order to spend the most time in their chosen destinations while others prefer to travel as slowly as possible. They feel they have plenty of time, and as most of them have already traveled around the world a couple of times there is no more rush. We fall into the latter category. We flew around the world three times before we understood that we are not busy and important. Nowadays we love to ride the slowest of trains and walk.

The mode of transportation is the most important to those global nomads who have their own vehicle. It is an important part of their lifestyle and for some it also offers accommodation and privacy.

For cyclists (13%), the bicycle is part of their identity. Some are fanatics, like Swiss Claude who considers cycling a true love story, *vélo story*, like they say in French. He regards his bicycle as man's best friend, before the dog. Cycling, in general, seems to be one of the most popular ways of traveling among global nomads. It is cheap and easy to travel, and it also keeps one fit. We talked with four cyclists and many others would have been available.

Some global nomads hitchhike (10%) short distances in

and around their destinations, but for three global nomads hitchhiking is their number one mode of transportation. Like cycling, it is loaded with various meanings. French hitchhiker Ludovic describes his round-the-world thumbing tour as the school of life: a school of persistence, patience, tolerance, open-mindedness, diplomacy, and resourcefulness.

For accommodation, global nomads use hotels, hostels, and guest houses, or they rent apartments or rooms. Some also sleep in their vehicles (10%) or in their tent. In addition, more than half (18) are members of a hospitality exchange. Some are super-users who also volunteer and work as ambassadors, like French nomad Michel. He stays in other peoples' homes nine out of ten nights when he is on the road. The rest (12) are not familiar with hospitality exchange or they had tried it, but were not satisfied with the experience. Some think that free accommodations are not worth the trouble since they have money to stay in hotels where they can enjoy privacy. For most active members, however, hospitality exchange offers more than just a free bed. They enjoy the opportunity to get to know locals and learn about their culture.

Formalized organizations are by no means necessary to experience hospitality. Cyclists, whose simple travel style makes them more approachable, are often invited to people's homes. "Cycling opens people's hearts," a Spanish cyclist sums up. Sometimes just asking where to pitch a tent or where to get drinking water, prompts the landowner to offer a room instead. Drivers may invite hitchhikers to stay in their home, and in Arab countries travelers are often asked to stay the night.

When necessary, global nomads sleep wherever: in squats (abandoned buildings), schools, stations, temples, beaches, forests, park benches, on the street, in gasoline stations, and in enclosed ATMs. One American is sleeping like a hobo: under the bridges, in tunnels, and in the forest. He chooses a place where people won't be able to see him sleeping, and at dawn he is up and back on the road before anyone knows he was there. Many are willing to give up modern comforts. They feel at home on the road regardless of the conditions.

Every now and then the travelers end up spending the night at a police station. Claude was arrested many times in Central and South America for cycling, and we once went to a police station in Gaborone, Botswana, after discovering hotels' prices were outrageously high. One nights' stay would have been more expensive than a night in Europe. The policemen kindly let us stay in the waiting room along with a few detained prostitutes.

The daily schedule of global nomads depends on various factors like: where and with whom they are with, and what the place has to offer. Global nomads prefer to keep their minds open to opportunities instead of planning and booking ahead. One thing is common with all global nomads, however. All of them want to explore their surroundings and meet locals, and when moving on, some unavoidable routines appear: next destinations must be pondered, accommodation has to be searched for, and friends and family need to be kept informed about one's whereabouts.

Cyclists share perhaps most routine days. They wake up early, have breakfast and start cycling. The spend the day in the saddle save meal breaks and meeting locals who often want to have their photos taken with a rare visitor, or they want to offer a cup of tea in their house. In the evening, it is time to find an accommodation, have a dinner, and rest. Those global nomads who work regularly do not separate work from free time—both are part of their lifestyle. Those traveling with their own vehicle are required to spend some time in repair and maintenance.

Although global nomads prefer an open schedule, not all of them are ready to give them up totally. To some extent, routines are needed to facilitate the process of settling down in a new place. Frequenting the same restaurant every day, for example, is a way to get to know people. For global nomads, routines are mainly about people, establishing connections and friendships. By getting to know locals, they make places familiar for themselves. Quoting hobo Andy, "Life cannot be a one-night stand."

Two thirds (60%) of the global nomads we interviewed believe wandering is a permanent lifestyle for them. At the time, they had traveled 4–30 years, and their journey had included various stages, both traveling and staying put in chosen destinations. Approximately one third (27%) consider their trip as a long sabbatical or a rite of passage after college or university. They want to explore the world before settling down. Plans concerning return are uncertain and they can be interpreted in various ways. None of the plans nor decisions—if such had been made—are permanent. They depend on various factors such as curiosity, energy, interests, family ties, friends, and financial situation.

How many years have they traveled?

Under 5 years	23% (7)
5–10 years	43% (13)
Over 10 years	33% (10)

The travel times varied between four and thirty years.

The average consumption of our global nomads was 644 dollars per person a month and varied between 210 dollars and 2,100 dollars in 2010. These sums included all costs: accommodation, food, travel, medical services, clothes, and also spare parts for the vehicle. Five of the nomads felt uneasy to reveal their costs.

Accommodation and intercontinental flights and ferries form the biggest part of costs for everyone. The majority of global nomads use hospitality exchange to cut costs. This way they also get to know a new place with a help of a local who can give tips for more economical restaurants, supermarkets, rooms or apartments to let, and help them learn the local culture of negotiation.

Wandering the world has made global nomads polyglots. Half of them speak more than four languages, the extremes being two and seven different languages. All speak English, which is the most common language among travelers. It was also necessary for the interviews we made. Other popular languages are European: Spanish, French, Portuguese, Italian, and German. Speakers of non-Western languages are surprisingly rare, although many know scraps of other languages including Turkish, Czech, Japanese, Chinese, Thai, and Indonesian. Two of the global nomads represent rare minority languages, Finnish and Hebrew. We haven't included ourselves in these statistics.

Linguistic abilities are considered vital as global nomads want to explore cultures from within. Without a common language, the traveler will always remain an outsider. The most avid language learners are solo travelers whose social life depends directly on their ability to communicate with locals. Couples are lazier, as we have noticed from our own experience. We have always each other as company, and as we already speak two rather useless languages, Finnish and Swedish, we have become reluctant to learn new languages that are limited to particular geographical areas.

Global nomads' other pastimes are varied. They read and write, exercise, hike, dive, meditate, and cook. Some like sightseeing while others avoid it. A few have volunteered in Third World countries, which—like hospitality exchange—offers a way to get to know locals and structure time whenever hanging out feels boring, meaningless, or inappropriate.

Even though global nomads make friends with people they meet around the world, maintaining those relationships is challenging. Friendships tend to fade over the years if friends are not regularly visited. It is the global nomad that is usually traveling away from friends and family while home owners stay at home and may not be willing to travel to maintain a friendship or family relations.

Families, in general, are used to the idea that a family member is traveling. Wanderlust is not a new trait in global nomads, but has probably shown itself since childhood. This rarely means, however, that the family wouldn't anxiously wait for and repeatedly ask about their return. Global nomads are often pressured to explain and justify their choices time and time again. Absence is hardest to endure in cultures that cherish tight family relations. French nomad Michel laughs sarcastically when we ask about his family's view: "They don't think about my lifestyle, they think about my retirement. The closer they are, the more they worry. Others are jealous."

Nomadic traveling excites outsiders and brings out both the good and the bad in people. Without exception, all global nomads have heard that someone else would like to live their lives, but are too afraid to do so. Global nomads explain the admiration away modestly. "My life sounds and seems so much more romantic than it really is," Captain Tor says. At the same time, some people feel pity for the homeless nomad who have to sleep on other people's floors and carry their possessions. These two reactions, admiration and disdain, have historically plagued the full-time traveler. Adventuring and vagrancy are stories that outsiders or casual observers use to try and make sense of an odd lifestyle. Which story is chosen, depends on the speaker and so in the end, these stories tell more about the observer and their values than the global nomads themselves.

To conclude this book, let it be noted that none of our fellow nomads call themselves 'global nomads.' However, they all found the term familiar and therefore it was chosen for this book. Nomadism means for them homelessness, spontaneity, pleasure taken in change and constant movement, and mastery of oneself. Many recalled that other people had called them nomads.

It is time to thank everyone for their invaluable help. We want to express our gratitude to our awesome colleagues who shared their time and thoughts with us. We wish you happy travels. Our quest, which we set when starting to write this book, continues. Päivi is conducting a research on global nomads for Tilburg University in the Netherlands, and I'm making a documentary film about them. Nomadism travels along with us everywhere we go.

This book was written on the road in Italy, Greece, Kenya, Tanzania, Zambia, Botswana, South-Africa, Malaysia, Thailand, Laos, the Philippines, China, Australia, Myanmar, India, and Morocco.

The Global Nomads

We have marked the ages of the global nomads at the time
of the interviews in 2010.

- Ajay, 24, Russia   traveliving.org
- Alberto, 39, Mexico
- Andy, 54, United States   www.hobotraveler.com
- Anick, 29, Canada   www.globestoppeuse.com
- Anthony, 35, Belgium   anthonyasael.com
- Barbara, 52, Canada/United States
- Ciro, 29, Portugal
- Claude, 50, Switzerland   www.yaksite.org
- George†, 31, United States
- Glen, 53, Great-Britain   glenswatman.blogspot.com
- Guilad, 32, Israel
- Guillermo†, 42, Spain
- Gustavo†, 51, Argentina†
- Helen, 29, Great-Britain
- Ingo, 36, Germany   www.ingoboltz.com
- Jeff, 25, United States
- Jens, 30, Germany

- Jérémy, 26, France   tour-du-monde-autostop.fr
- Jukka, 27, Finland   jukkasalminen.com
- Ludovic, 32, France   www.ludovichubler.com
- Maria, 32, Russia   traveliving.org
- Max, 39, United States   xonlife.com
- Michel, 47, France
- Phoenix, 49, United States
- Rita, 72, United States   www.ritagoldengelman.com
- Scott, 33, United States
- Stefan, 47, Austria
- Suzan, 54, United States   globalgypsycollection.com
- Taro, 27, Japan   sorapiz.xii.jp
- Tor, 61, United States   www.tor.cc

† Pseudonym. Name and/or country have been changed to protect the identity of the interviewee as per his request.

Select Bibliography

Aneziri, Sophia 2009, 'World travelers: The Associations of Artists of Dionysus,' in Richard Hunter and Ian Rutherford (eds.), *Wandering Poets in Ancient Greek Culture: Travel, Locality and Pan-Hellenism.* Cambridge: Cambridge University Press, pp. 217–236.

Azarya, Victor 2001, 'The Nomadic Factor in Africa: Dominance or Marginality,' in Anatoly M. Khazanov and André Wink (eds.), *Nomads in the Sedentary World.* Richmond: Curzon Press, pp. 250–284.

Beier, A.L. 2004, *The Problem of the Poor in Tudor and Early Stuart England* [1983], ebook, last accessed April 1, 2012 from <http://www.taylorandfrancis.com/books/details/9780203392782/>.

Bergreen, Lawrence 2007, *Marco Polo: From Venice to Xanadu*, audio book, read by Paul Boehmer. New

York: RandomHouse Audio.

Besserman, Perle and Manfred Steger 1991, *Crazy Clouds: Zen Radicals, Rebels & Reformers*. Massachusetts and London: Shambala Publications.

Calhoun, Craig 2002, 'The Class Consciousness of Frequent Travelers: Toward a Critique of Actually Existing Cosmopolitanism,' in *The South Atlantic Quarterly* 101(4), Fall 2002, pp. 869–897.

Caner, Daniel 2002, *Wandering, Begging Monks: Spiritual Authority and the Promotion of Monasticism in Late Antiquity*. Berkeley and Los Angeles: University of California Press.

Chatwin, Bruce 1997, *Anatomy of Restlessness: Uncollected Writings*. London: Picador.

Cohen, Erik 1973, 'Nomads from Affluence: Notes on the Phenomenon of Drifter-tourism,' in *International Journal of Comparative Sociology*, 14(1–2), pp. 89–103.

DePastino, Todd 2003, *The Citizen Hobo: How a Century of Homelessness Shaped America*. Chicago and London: The University of Chicago Press.

Dionne, Craig and Steve Mentz (eds.) 2006, *Rogues and Early Modern English Culture*. Michigan: The University of Michigan Press.

Euben, Roxanne L. 2006, *Journeys to the Other Shore: Muslim and Western Travellers in Search of Knowledge*. Princeton and Oxford: Princeton University Press.

Grant, Richard 2003, *Ghost Riders: Travels with American Nomads*. London: Abacus.

Hacking, Ian 1998, *Mad Travelers: Reflections On the Reality of Transient Mental Illnesses*. Charlottesville and London: University Press of Virginia.

Hausner, Sondra L. 2007, *Wandering with the Sadhus: Ascetics in Hindu Himalayas*. Bloomington, Indiana: Indiana University Press.

Heine, Steven and Wright, Dale S. 2000, *The Koan: Texts*

and Contexts in Zen Buddhism. Oxford: Oxford
University Press.
Hunter, Richard and Rutherford, Ian (eds.) 2009,
*Wandering Poets in Ancient Greek Culture: Travel,
Locality and Pan-Hellenism*. Cambridge: Cambridge
University Press.
Khazanov, Anatoly M. and André Wink (eds.) 2001,
Nomads in the Sedentary World. Richmond: Curzon
Press.
Linnaues, Carl 2003, *Linnaeus' Philosophia* Botanica [1751].
Oxford and New York: Oxford University Press.
London, Jack 1907, *The Road*, ebook, last accessed
April 6, 2012 from <http://www.gutenberg.org/
ebooks/14658>.
Orwell, George 1986, *Down and Out in Paris and London*
[1933], audio book, read by Patrick Tull. Prince
Frederick, Maryland: Recorded Books.
Rousseau, Jean-Jacques 1979, *Émile: or on Education* [1762],
translated by Allan Bloom. New York: Basic Books.
Sans toit ni loi, 1985, motion picture, Ciné Tamaris, Films
A2 and Ministére de la culture, distributed by MK2
Diffusion, France.
Thompson, Carl S. 2007, *The Suffering Traveller and the
Romantic Imagination*. Oxford: Clarendon Press.
Torpey, John 2000, *The Invention of the Passport:
Surveillance, Citizenship and the State*. Cambridge:
Cambridge University Press.
Worthington, Ian 2005 (ed.), *Alexander the Great: A
Reader*, ebook, last accessed April 12, 2012 from
<http://www.ebookstore.tandf.co.uk/html/moreinfo.
asp?bookid=536895716>.

Made in the USA
Charleston, SC
03 August 2013